Series / Number 07-076

LONGITUDINAL RESEARCH

SCOTT MENARD
Institute of Behavioral Science
University of Colorado, Boulder

SAGE PUBLICATIONS
The International Professional Publishers
Newbury Park   London   New Delhi

For information address:

 SAGE Publications, Inc.
2455 Teller Road
Newbury Park, California 91320

SAGE Publications Ltd.
6 Bonhill Street
London EC2A 4PU
United Kingdom

SAGE Publications India Pvt. Ltd.
M-32 Market
Greater Kailash I
New Delhi 110 048 India

Printed in the United States of America

International Standard Book Number 0-8039-3753-9

Library of Congress Catalog Card No. 90-20103

FIRST PRINTING, 1991

Sage Production Editor: Judith Hunter

When citing a university paper, please use the proper form. Remember to cite the current Sage University paper series title and include the paper number. One of the following formats can be adapted (depending on the style manual used):

(1) WELLER, S. C., & ROMNEY, A. K. (1990) Metric Scaling: Correspondence Analysis. Sage University Paper Series on Quantitative Applications in the Social Sciences, 07-075. Newbury Park, CA: Sage.

OR

(2) Weller, S. C., & Romney, A. K. (1990). *Metric scaling: Correspondence analysis* (Sage University Paper series on Quantitative Applications in the Social Sciences, series no. 07-075). Newbury Park, CA: Sage.

CONTENTS

Series Editor's Introduction   1

1. **Introduction   3**
   Definition   4

2. **The Purposes of Longitudinal Research   5**
   Age, Period, and Cohort Effects   6
   Causal Relationships   17
   Serendipity and Intentionality in Longitudinal Data   20

3. **Designs for Longitudinal Data Collection   22**
   Not-Quite-Longitudinal Designs   22
   Total Population Designs   24
   Repeated Cross-Sectional Designs   26
   Revolving Panel Designs   28
   Longitudinal Panel Designs   29
   Other Variations   30

4. **Issues in Longitudinal Research   31**
   Genesis Versus Prediction   32
   Changes in Measurement Over Time   33
   Panel Attrition   36
   Repeated Measurement and Panel Conditioning   38
   Respondent Recall   39
   The Costs of Longitudinal Research   42

5. **Longitudinal Analysis   44**
   Conceptualizing and Measuring Change   44
   Describing Patterns of Change   49
   Temporal and Causal Order   53
   Causal Analysis   59
   Longitudinal Versus Cross-Sectional Data and Analysis   66

Notes   71

References   73

About the Author   81

SERIES EDITOR'S INTRODUCTION

Longitudinal research concerns the collection and analysis of data over time. In principle, the same variables are measured on the same units of analysis for at least two time periods. As such, it marks itself off from *cross-sectional* research, where the data are gathered at one point in time. A typical cross-sectional example is the public opinion survey, with a sample of respondents (from, say, the voting population) interviewed more or less contemporaneously. In contrast, a longitudinally designed survey might interview this same sample of voters twice, at two different election periods (thus forming a two-wave *panel study*). Because both designs — longitudinal and cross-sectional — are non-experimental, questions of causal inference are always quite complex. However, longitudinal work offers a major advantage in that regard, since the temporal ordering of a relationship may be argued with more certitude. That is, when Y is shown actually to occur after X, we gain confidence that X "causes" or somehow "influences" Y. Let a hypothetical example clarify this point.

Suppose Dr. Mary White, criminal justice scholar, wishes to test the hypothesis that "aging makes people more fearful of crime." Therefore, she conducts a victimization survey of 1000 randomly chosen Gotham City adults, all interviewed in a month period (labeled time *t1*). Analyzing the responses, she finds X (age of respondent) strongly correlates with Y (a fear of crime index). Nevertheless, she avoids the simple conclusion that aging makes people more fearful of crime. Instead, she suspects that the relationship between X and Y is spurious, a product of the common relationship of actual crime experience (Z) to both. That is, older people are more likely to have been victims of crime, and those who have been victims are more likely to be fearful. Dr. White now conducts two other surveys (adding more items on specific recent victimizations) with the same sample, at *t2* and six months later at *t3*. She finds a strong correlation between earlier crime experience (at *t2*) and later fear of crime (at *t3*). Moreover, this correlation remains strong within each age cohort (young, middle, old). These panel results favor the

1

conclusion that victimization itself, rather than the aging process, leads to fear of crime. Of course, other problems have yet to be considered — respondent attrition, recall bias, possible spuriousness from other sources. However, the panel study has moved Prof. White closer to sorting out the determinants of fear of crime.

The above illustration of a longitudinal design was inspired by one of the many well-chosen real data examples provided here by Dr. Menard. He has selected carefully from youth surveys, crime surveys, election surveys, and fertility studies, to name a few. These examples help the research worker understand the methods for gathering longitudinal data, a topic engagingly discussed in the first part of the monograph. Then, issues in the problems of longitudinal analysis are introduced. For instance, the knotty question of how to measure change — differences, residuals, or lags — is posed. But, Dr. Menard gives the reader an appreciation of opportunities as well as difficulties, and outlines several promising analytic strategies. After finishing this monograph, students should feel encouraged to launch their own longitudinal research project.

— Michael S. Lewis-Beck

LONGITUDINAL RESEARCH

SCOTT MENARD

1. INTRODUCTION

Longitudinal data have been collected at the national level for more than 300 years, beginning with the periodic censuses taken by New France (Canada) and continued in Quebec from 1665 until 1754. These were not the first censuses, but they did represent the first periodic collection of census data, as opposed to single isolated censuses taken at irregular intervals. The latter began as early as the Israelite census of 1491 B.C. (Thomlinson, 1976). Other periodic censuses that have continued to the present include those of Sweden since 1749, Norway and Denmark since 1769, and the United States since 1790. The United States is exceptional among nations because it has longitudinal census data from the first decade of its existence as a nation up to the present. At the individual level, Baltes and Nesselroade (1979) and Wall and Williams (1970) cite collection of longitudinal data (primarily case study and biographical data) as early as 1759. Long-term studies of childhood development involving multiple subjects flourished in the United States after World War I, and a broad array of longitudinal studies in the social and behavioral sciences has been undertaken in the 1970s and 1980s. The proliferation of longitudinal research attests to its perceived importance by both researchers and major funding agencies. When questions have been raised about the value of longitudinal research, those questions have more often addressed the quality of the research in terms of design and analysis than the value of longitudinal research in principle for answering questions that cannot adequately be addressed by other types of data-collection designs and analysis.

The use of longitudinal data and methods has recently become quite fashionable, and for many, longitudinal research is touted as a panacea for establishing temporal order, measuring change, and making stronger causal interpretations. Although there are indeed certain advantages associated with these methods, there are offsetting costs and difficulties. Longitudinal research may not always be necessary even for establishing causal order

AUTHOR'S NOTE: *I would like to thank Delbert S. Elliott and two anonymous reviewers for their suggestions, and Zeke Little for the original graphics used in this manuscript.*

(Davis, 1985; Blalock, 1962), particularly when the temporal order of variables is known in advance (for example, biological or genetic characteristics such as sex, race, and age), and longitudinal data are certainly not a cure for weak research design and data analysis.

Definition

In this discussion of longitudinal research, I use the term *longitudinal* to describe not a single method, but a family of methods (Zazzo, 1967). This family of methods is best understood by contrasting longitudinal research with cross-sectional research. In *pure cross-sectional research*, measurement occurs once for each individual, subject, country, or *case* in the study; the measurement of each item, concept, or *variable* applies to a single time interval or *period;* and the measurement of each variable for each case occurs within a sufficiently narrow span of time (ideally it would occur simultaneously for each variable for each case) that the measurements may be regarded as *contemporaneous*, that is, occurring within the same period for all variables and for all cases. Depending on the particular study, a period may be defined in terms of seconds, days, months, years, or (in principle) geological epochs. In the social and behavioral sciences, periods typically vary from minutes in some laboratory experiments to years in some cross-national research.

Longitudinal research must be defined in terms of both the data and the methods of analysis that are used in the research. Longitudinal research is research in which (a) data are collected for each item or variable for two or more distinct time periods; (b) the subjects or cases analyzed are the same or at least comparable from one period to the next; and (c) the analysis involves some comparison of data between or among periods. At a bare minimum, any truly longitudinal design would permit the measurement of differences or change in a variable from one period to another. According to this definition, several types of research may be regarded as longitudinal. In one, data may be collected *at* two or more distinct periods, *for* those distinct periods, on the same set of cases and variables in each period. This is a *prospective panel design*. Alternatively, data may be collected *at* a single period, *for* several periods, usually including the period that ends with the time at which the data are collected. This *retrospective panel design* may be identical to a prospective panel design in every respect except the number of times data collection actually takes place and the length of the recall period required of respondents. In both panel designs the cases and variables remain the same from one period to the next. A third possibility is to collect data on the same set of variables for (and perhaps *at*) two or more periods, but to include nonidentical (but comparable) cases in each period. In this *repeated cross-sectional design*, the data for each period may be regarded as a separate cross-section, but because the cases are comparable from one period to another (for example, by using probability samples drawn from the same population), we may make comparisons between or among periods. These different types of longitudinal designs are presented in greater detail in Chapter 3.

Baltes and Nesselroade (1979) and Wall and Williams (1970) have suggested narrower definitions of longitudinal research that would exclude all except prospective panel designs, but they acknowledge (Baltes and Nesselroade, 1979: 4; Wall and Williams, 1970: 14) that there is no consensus on this point. Baltes and Nesselroade suggest that longitudinal research may need to be defined within the context of a specific discipline. For developmental studies in psychology, it may be appropriate to consider only longitudinal panel designs, but in other disciplines this seems too restrictive. Our reasons for using a broader definition of longitudinal research are, first, the lack of consensus regarding what constitutes longitudinal research, and second, the usefulness of considering the different features of the full range of methods used in collecting data for different time periods.

The remainder of this monograph is organized as follows. In Chapter 2, I discuss the purposes of longitudinal research and the difficulties involved in separating historical and developmental changes. Chapter 3 presents and discusses basic designs for the collection of longitudinal data. In Chapter 4, I discuss issues that may affect the quality of longitudinal data. Finally, a brief introduction to and overview of methods of longitudinal analysis is presented in Chapter 5.

2. THE PURPOSES OF LONGITUDINAL RESEARCH

Longitudinal research serves two primary purposes: to describe patterns of change, and to establish the direction (positive or negative, and from Y to X or from X to Y) and magnitude (a relationship of magnitude zero indicating the absence of a causal relationship) of causal relationships. Change is typically measured with reference to one of two continua: chronological time (hereafter simply *time*) or *age*. Time is measured externally to the cases or subjects being studied (e.g., 2:22 P.M., 28 August 1989). Age is measured internally, relative to the subject or case under study (e.g., 38 years, 7 months, 26 days, 8 hours, and 27 minutes since birth). In one sense, age represents biological time for human subjects. The choice of time or age as the underlying continuum may be important, and for some purposes it may be useful to consider both in the same analysis. Also important is the distinction between age-related differences when age is measured cross-sectionally (differences between subjects who are 40 years old and subjects who are 50 years old in 1980) and age measured longitudinally (differences between subjects who are 40 years old in 1980 and those same subjects when they are 50 years old in 1990). When age is measured cross-sectionally, the differences between variables for 40-year-olds and 50-year-olds may be interpreted as differences *between* birth cohorts or age groups at a particular time. When age is measured longitudinally, the differences may be interpreted as *developmental* differences *within* a cohort or age group over time.

Age, Period, and Cohort Effects

The distinction between time and age as conceptually distinct continua along which change may be measured can pose serious problems of interpretation in the study of change. To understand these problems, and to lay a firm foundation for discussing the measurement of historical and developmental change, it is necessary to discuss the distinctions among age, period, and cohort as variables and as units of analysis.

The demographic definition of a cohort is provided by Glenn (1977: 8): "A cohort is defined as those people within a geographically or otherwise delineated population who experienced the same significant life event within a given period of time." A similar definition is offered by Ryder (1965). Both Glenn and Ryder note that although the term *cohort* is almost always used to refer to *birth* cohorts (those born in a particular year or period), one may also define cohorts in terms of year of marriage or divorce, year of retirement or first employment, or year of occurrence of any number of events other than birth. Graetz (1987) uses the term *event cohort* to describe cohorts other than birth cohorts.

Suppose that we want to test the hypothesis that people become politically more conservative as they grow older. One approach would be to do a survey of individuals of different ages in a given year, ask questions about their political attitudes, and compare younger respondents with older respondents. If the older respondents reported being more politically conservative than the younger respondents, we might conclude that people do become more conservative as they get older, but there is a plausible alternative hypothesis. Perhaps those in our sample who are older and more conservative were just as conservative when they were younger, and perhaps our younger, less conservative respondents will remain less conservative as they grow older. In other words, cross-sectional differences by age may be confused with differences that result not from age but from the effects of membership in different birth cohorts. Put another way, different life experiences at certain, perhaps relatively young, ages may have long-lasting effects on the attitudes of different individuals.

Suppose now that instead of doing a cross-sectional study, we select a single birth cohort and interview a sample of respondents from this cohort every 5 or 10 years until they die. At the end of our study, if we found that respondents were more conservative when they were older, we might conclude that political conservatism increases with age. Again, however, there is a plausible alternative hypothesis. It is possible that there is no real difference among age groups in any one year, but that everyone, young and old, is becoming more conservative over time, for reasons that have nothing to do with age. This would suggest an effect of history, specific to years or periods rather than to ages. Put another way, contemporary events may have an immediate effect on political conservatism, regardless of age. The problem of a period difference does not arise in the cross-sectional study because there is only one period. The problem of a cohort difference does not arise in a longitudinal study because there is only one cohort.

Since neither a cross-sectional study nor a single-cohort longitudinal study can eliminate both cohort membership and period effects as rival hypotheses, it would seem logical to combine the two approaches and use a multiple-year, multiple-cohort design. Then we could control for both cohort membership and period in examining the effect of age on political conservatism. The problem with this is that if we assume that the effects of age, period, and cohort membership are all linear, controlling for any two variables controls for the third as well. This is because age, period, and cohort membership, as measured here, are linearly dependent; each is a linear function of the other two. Mathematically,

cohort (year of birth) = period (year) − age (years since birth).

Again we are stymied in our attempt to test the hypothesis that political conservatism increases as a result of age. Including all three (age, period, and cohort) in a regression equation, for example, would result in perfect collinearity. Any age effect we find without controlling for both period and cohort may, with equal plausibility, be attributable to the combined or separate effects of cohort membership and trends over time. This problem, along with other problems in cohort analysis (sampling, sample mortality, and so on) is discussed in some detail in Glenn (1977).

Linear Dependence and the Conceptual Status of Cohorts. Attempts have been made to overcome the problem of linear dependence among age, period, and birth cohort. These include the use of dummy variable regression analysis with certain restrictive assumptions about the parameters in the model (Mason et al., 1973) and the recombination and *a priori* elimination of one or more of the three types of effects (Palmore, 1978). These attempts, particularly the dummy variable regression model, have generated considerable methodological controversy (Baltes et al., 1979; Glenn, 1976 and 1977; Knoke and Hout, 1976; Mason et al., 1973; Rodgers, 1982a and 1982b; Smith et al., 1982) regarding the plausibility of the assumptions and the consequences of violating the assumptions needed to deal with the problem of linear dependence among age, period, and birth cohort. In addition, these methods do not solve the problem of linear dependence, because the Mason et al. (1973) model assumes that not all of the effects are linear, and in Palmore's method, one effect must be eliminated *a priori*. The use of such assumptions could as easily be built into ordinary least-squares regression models.

Note that the problem of linear dependence applies to birth cohorts, but not necessarily to other types of cohorts. To the extent that an event is not dependent on age or period, an event cohort based on that event is not linearly dependent on age or period. In some cases, then, linear dependence may be eliminated *a priori*. A second and more fundamental point regarding age, period, and cohort effects is that cohorts, as aggregates of individuals, are units of analysis, cases for study. It is in this sense that the term cohort is used by Ryder (1965) and implemented in some studies of cohort effects (e.g., Carlson, 1979; Lloyd et al., 1987; Wetzel et al., 1987). Baltes et al. (1979) discuss three possible conceptualizations of cohort (error or disturbance; dimension of generalization; theoretical and process variable), one of which (dimension of generalization) corresponds to the use of cohorts as units of analysis, rather than as theoretical variables. Even some studies that use cohort as an explanatory variable also recognize cohort as a unit of analysis (e.g., Wright and Maxim, 1987).

Cohorts are aggregates of individuals (cases). As cases, they may be analyzed in the same way as other cases (individuals, cities, nations). In social science research, cohorts, like other aggregate cases, have measurable characteristics, some of which are inherently aggregate in nature (size, sex ratio, ethnic composition) and others of which are summations (total number of arrests) or averages (median lifetime income) of the individuals who are included in the cohort. By contrast, we do not measure aggregate characteristics of ages or periods, as such, but we may measure aggregate characteristics of cases *during* a particular age or period. Ages and periods are aggregates of time, variables rather than units of analysis. They may be used to delimit the cases for analysis in a particular study, but they are not themselves typically employed as units of analysis in social research.

Age, period, and birth cohort, respectively, answer the questions "how old are you?" "what year is it?" and "in what year were you born?" The answer to the question "how old are you?" may explain some forms of behavior: Wetting one's pants is most common in infancy, illegal behavior tends to be highest in adolescence, and retirement is most common after age 65. Age provides a *developmental* explanation for behavior. The answer to the question "what year is it?" may also help explain some forms of behavior: In the United States, use of illicit drugs was more common after 1960 than before, and overt racial discrimination was more common before 1960 than after. Period provides an explanation, or at least a weak proxy for an explanation (Hobcraft et al., 1982), that is *historical* in nature and that may help identify those historical events that are most plausible as explanations for a given behavior.

There are two ways in which the answer to the question "in what year were your born?" may be used to explain behavior. The first is what we may call Oriental Astrological Theory: Individuals born in certain years have certain characteristics by virtue of having been born in that year. For example, according to Oriental astrology, women born in the year of the fiery horse (which recurs every 60 years) have a propensity to murder their husbands. For most social scientists, this is a rather unsatisfactory approach to explaining homicide; it does, however, have an impact either on actual fertility or on the reported (but not necessarily true) birth date of women in Japan, as documented by the Population Reference Bureau (1989). Alternatively, the year in which one is born explains one's behavior in terms of how old one was (development) in a particular year or during particular events (history). In other words, the effect of birth cohort, measured as year of birth, may serve as a proxy for the interaction of the effects of age and period.

Cohort Effects: Reconceptualization and Replacement. One approach to cohort effects, then, is to regard them as the interaction of age and period effects. An alternative would be to assume that it is not cohort membership itself, but rather some characteristic or set of characteristics associated with the birth cohort that produced the apparent cohort effect. The problem then becomes one of identifying the appropriate characteristic or set of characteristics of the cohort, a theoretical rather than a methodological problem.

One solution to this problem has potentially broad applicability: For cohort, measured as year of birth, substitute the number of individuals born in a birth cohort, or cohort size. According to Ryder (1965), "A cohort's size relative to its neighbors is a persistent and compelling feature of its lifetime environment." Mason et al. (1973) note that all three variables, age, period, and cohort, are proxies for unmeasured variables, and they indicate that "if cohort size is the variable which causes differentiation in the context of a specific substantive problem, then, if size measurements can be constructed, it is unnecessary to include cohorts as such in the specification because the preferred variable is available." They also note that use of cohort size eliminates the estimability problem for which their dummy variable regression model was constructed, and makes the results of the analysis less tentative. Hobcraft et al. (1982) and Rodgers (1982a) raise similar points. Ryder (1965) notes that size is only one of several characteristics that may be used to differentiate cohorts from one another; however, cohort size is the characteristic that has played the most important role in research since the publication in 1968 of Easterlin's work regarding the impact of cohort size on the labor force, and his subsequent work, published in 1980, regarding the impact of cohort size on a variety of social problems, including unemployment, divorce, and crime (Easterlin, 1987).

The point of all this is that cohort, measured as year of birth, has sometimes been used when cohort size or some other cohort characteristic (or a nonlinear interaction term involving age and period) would have been more conceptually or theoretically appropriate for studying age, period, and cohort effects. This may stem at least in part from a failure to recognize that age, period, and cohort have qualitatively different conceptual statuses. Although, as noted above, cohort membership may be treated as an explanatory variable from a purely methodological viewpoint, it is not generally appropriate, theoretically and substantively, to do so. Age and period are more appropriate as explanatory variables, age more so than period (Hobcraft et al., 1982). Ideally, one would eliminate period and cohort and replace them with the variables for which they act as proxies in any causal analysis.

In the analysis of developmental or historical change, the use of multiple-year, multiple-cohort designs, coupled with appropriate operationalization of age, period, and cohort effects (i.e., the use of cohort characteristics or of a nonlinear age-period interaction) would allow us to test whether age had an effect on political attitudes, net of period effects and cohort membership. Some solution of the problem of confounding among age, period, and cohort effects, whether theoretical (e.g., use of cohort size based on the work of Esterlin and others, or *a priori* elimination of the possibility of a cohort effect) or methodological (e.g., use of the Mason et al. dummy variable regression technique) needs to be found before age effects can be inferred in any study. In the example of political conservatism, it may be theoretically reasonable to eliminate cohort membership as an influence on political attitudes, or to assume (on theoretical grounds) that any effect of cohort membership operates through cohort size (or some other cohort characteristic). Once this is done, it becomes possible to estimate separate age (developmental) and period (historical) effects on political attitudes. Note that developmental, historical, and cohort membership effects cannot be clearly separated without longitudinal data.

Period Effects: Changes Over Time. Once one has dealt with the issue of separating age, period, and cohort effects, it becomes possible to examine changes as they occur over time. Typically, this will mean either ignoring cohort effects or representing them in terms of cohort characteristics such as cohort size. In addition, if we are concerned only with changes over chronological time (historical changes) and not with changes over age (developmental changes), we must either be certain that age is entirely irrelevant, or include age as an explanatory variable, or control for age by making age-specific comparisons.

One concern of longitudinal research is the simple description of changes in values of variables over time. At the individual level of analysis, this may include changes in religious beliefs, political conservatism, or use of alcohol. Most often it is necessary to consider the possibility that change at the individual level may represent a developmental rather than a historical trend. At an aggregate level, we may use changes in rates of crime or victimization, in worker productivity or in per capita gross national product, in Scholastic Aptitude Test (SAT) scores, or in infant mortality rates, as *social indicators*[1] of progress or decline in meeting basic social needs or achieving desirable social goals. At this level it may be possible to control for the effects of age. Infant mortality is already age-specific (although the age of the mother may affect the likelihood of the infant's death before age one), and the SAT is taken primarily by individuals aged 16-18. Age is thus controlled completely or to a large extent for these measures. Rates of crime and victimization are sensitive to the age distribution of the population (e.g., Chilton and Spielberger, 1971; Skogan, 1976), and it would be appropriate to control for age composition in evaluating the evidence for historical trends for these variables. Per capita gross national product may be sensitive to the age-dependency ratio (the ratio of those under age 15 plus those over age 65 to those ages 16-64), and it is also possible that worker productivity is sensitive to the age distribution of workers, but if these change slowly or remain fairly constant over the periods for which the data are collected, it may be possible to ignore changes in age or age distribution as sources of variation in period trends.

One of the safest ways to approach the study of trends over time is to use age-specific comparisons. In an age-specific comparison, only those cases of a certain age in one year are compared with cases of the same age in some subsequent year. The age may represent a single year (e.g., age 15) or a range of years (e.g., over age 65), and separate comparisons may be made for all possible ages or age groups. For example, Gold and his associates (Gold and Reimer, 1975; Williams and Gold, 1972) examined rates of self-reported delinquency among national probability samples of 13- to 16-year-olds in a repeated cross-sectional design, and found little evidence of change from 1967 to 1972. Menard (1987a) obtained similar results for national probability samples of 15- to 17-year-olds from 1976 to 1980. His data were taken from a prospective panel study, and in order to separate age and period effects, he used only 15- to 17-year-olds (the only ages for which data were available in all five years) in each year. Covey and Menard (1987, 1988) examined trends in victimization and trends in arrests for those over age 65 and found that rates of arrests were generally increasing and rates of victimization were generally decreasing among this older age group. In each of the above-cited studies, controlling for age produced relatively unambiguous evidence for the existence or absence of trends over time. Without such controls for age, it may be difficult to ascertain whether changes are historical or developmental in nature, even if the entire population is used instead of a sample. Chilton and Spielberger (1971) examined changes in official crime rates and found that much of the apparent change over time (what appeared on the surface to be a change in behavior) was attributable to changes in the age structure, or more specifically, to changes in the percentage of the population in the adolescent ages. Individual studies will vary, but in general it is appropriate to consider the possibility that apparent period trends may actually be attributable to changes in age (at the individual level) or age composition (at the aggregate level).

Temporal Trends in Relationships Between Variables. Another concern of longitudinal research is the examination of changes, not in values or levels of variables over time, but in *relationships* between or among variables over time. It is one thing, for example, to say that mortality has been declining for more than two centuries. It is another to indicate that in the early stages of mortality decline, reductions in mortality were achieved primarily by public health measures (sanitation, access to safe drinking water, pasteurization, and so forth) and medicine played little if any role, but in the later stages of the decline, advances in medicine (inoculation, antibiotics) rather than public health measures were responsible for mortality declines (McKeown, 1976; McKeown and Record, 1962; McNeill, 1976).

In the context of examining changes in the strength or patterns of relationships over time, one important concern is the replication of previous results with new data. Elliott et al. (1989) used data from successive years to test a theoretical model of delinquent behavior on a set of dependent variables that included delinquency, drug use, and mental health problems. In the initial test, the results indicated that the model did a good job of explaining delinquency and drug use, but a poorer job of explaining mental health problems. Using data from the same subjects, measured one year later, Elliott et al. successfully replicated the results of the first test. The ability to replicate results from one period to the next (in effect, an indicator of reliability of results) provides more support for the model than would a single test, without replication.

Replication is not always successful, and evidence of changes in strength or patterns of relationships over time may alert the researcher to real changes in relationships or to methodological problems such as instability or unreliability of measurement, or misspecification of a causal model. Menard (1987b) tested a model of fertility on 85 less developed countries for the periods 1970 and 1980. The overall patterns for the two periods were very similar, but relationships involving family planning program effort changed from 1970 to 1980, usually in the direction of weaker relationships. Other than this change, the model for the two periods produced almost identical results. As indicated by Menard, these changes may have reflected changes in the measurement of family planning program effort, but the strong relationship (Pearson's $r = .83$) between family planning program effort as measured in the two periods seemed more suggestive of a real change in the strength of the relationship than of unreliability in measurement. Neither the possibility of instability or unreliability of measurement nor the overall consistency of the model from one period to another could have been documented without replication.

Age Effects: Life Cycle and Developmental Changes. Baltes and Nesselroade (1979) listed five objectives or rationales for longitudinal (or more specifically, in their case, prospective panel) research: (1) direct identification of intraindividual change, i.e., whether individuals change from one period to another; (2) direct identification of interindividual similarities or differences in intraindividual change, i.e., whether individuals change in the same or different ways; (3) analysis of interrelationships in behavioral change, i.e., whether certain changes are correlated with each other; (4) analysis of causes or determinants of intraindividual change, i.e., why individuals change from one period to another; and (5) analysis of causes or determinants of interindividual similarities or differences in intraindividual change, i.e., why different individuals change in different ways from one period to another. All of these objectives are concerned with patterns of developmental change, specifically at the individual level, although they are easily extended to aggregate levels (groups, organizations, cities, nations). At the individual level, intraindividual changes may include things people think (becoming more politically conservative), things they do (becoming employed, changing jobs, retiring), or things that are done to them (being arrested or being robbed). In the study of intraindividual change, age serves as a proxy for physiological changes and exposure to social influences (Hobcraft et al., 1982) that may be difficult or costly to measure directly.

For some purposes it may be reasonable to draw simple inferences about intraindividual change from cross-sectional data. For example, from cross-sectional data on rates of arrest and childbearing by age, we may reasonably infer that one's likelihood of being arrested or of having a baby is practically nonexistent before age 7, increases in adolescence and early adulthood, and diminishes substantially after age 65. There would seem to be little chance that these age-related differences may be explained by period effects or cohort characteristics. On the other hand, it would not be safe to infer that people become more conservative and less educated as they get older, based on cross-sectional data. As noted earlier, age differences in political attitudes at a particular period may reflect either changes in attitudes with age, or constancy in attitudes over the life cycle coupled with differences in attitudes between cohorts. If older people have less education than younger people, it is not because they become "de-educated"; a more plausible explanation is that educational attainment has increased over time (a period effect), resulting in differences in the average educational level of successive cohorts.

The use of cross-sectional data to study the relationship between age and behavior amounts to the construction of a synthetic cohort, a practice common in the demographic study of mortality and fertility. Life expectancy and period total fertility rates, for example, are based on the use of cross-sectional mortality and fertility rates, but are extrapolated by insurance companies (in the case of life expectancy) and others to describe what may happen to an individual or a cohort of individuals as they grow older. As Shryock and

Siegel (1976: 324) caution, the utility of synthetic cohort measures depends on the extent to which they reflect the actual experience of real cohorts (something that can be evaluated only with longitudinal research on cohorts). In some cases, cross-sectional and longitudinal data may lead to very different conclusions about developmental patterns. For example, Greenberg (1985), using officially reported crime, and Menard and Elliott (1990a), using self-reported delinquency, both found that cross-sectional and longitudinal data may produce different conclusions about the precise relationship between age and illegal behavior. In part, the differences between the longitudinal and cross-sectional results may be attributable to cohort size effects (Elliott et al., 1989: 107-109; Menard and Elliott, 1990b).

A more compelling need for longitudinal data arises if we wish to study "career" patterns of behavior. The most obvious application of this is in the study of labor market careers, from initial job entry through patterns of promotion, job change, job loss, and eventually either retirement or death. Closely related to this is the study of status attainment careers, which includes consideration of educational attainment as well as occupational status and income (e.g., Blau and Duncan, 1966). Other applications of the "career" perspective include marital histories (e.g., Becker et al., 1977), educational attainment and the process of learning (e.g., Heyns, 1978), and criminal careers (e.g., Blumstein et al., 1986). Such studies have in common a concern with patterns of entry, continuity, and exit from the behavior upon which the career is based, and with the correlates and potential causes associated with changes or discontinuities in the behavior (unemployment and obtaining a new job; divorce and remarriage; dropout and reentry in education; suspension and resumption of criminal behavior). It is only with longitudinal data, and more specifically panel data, that many of the questions regarding developmental career patterns may be answered.

Longitudinal data are also important in experimental research and evaluation research. Most experimental designs and quasi-experimental designs are inherently longitudinal, with measurement occurring both before (pretest) and after (posttest) the experimental treatment or intervention is administered (Campbell and Stanley, 1963), in order to ascertain whether differences at the posttest are attributable to the treatment or to preexisting differences between treatment and control groups. In experimental designs, even when a pretest is not used, the researcher assumes that the randomization of the assignment of subjects to different treatments produces groups that either do not differ on any important variable, or whose deviations from equality are subject to known statistical distributions. Even a posttest-only experimental design thus includes a critical longitudinal assumption, namely that a difference between the experimental and control groups at the posttest represents a change from the pretest, at which it is assumed, without possibility of proof or disproof, that there is little or no difference between the experimental and the control groups. Similarly, pretest or baseline data are often collected in evaluation research (Rossi and Freeman, 1989). The absence of pretest or baseline data has the effect of rendering uncertain whether differences after some treatment or intervention may be wholly attributable to the treatment or intervention, or to preexisting differences between the group that did and the group that did not receive the treatment or intervention.

Developmental Trends in Relationships Among Variables. Parallel to the earlier concern with examining changes in the strength or pattern of relationships from one period to another, we may want to examine changes in the strength or pattern of relationships from one age to another. Here again the issue of whether to base the comparison on cross-sectional (intercohort) or longitudinal (intracohort) data may arise, and as before the decision hinges on whether we are concerned with how well the developmental changes are reflected in the cross-sectional data. If longitudinal data are used, the issue of whether any change that occurs is attributable to age, period, or cohort effects must again be considered.

In a study of 341 adolescent boys in New Jersey, LaGrange and White (1985) found that for older (age 18) and younger (age 12) adolescent boys, only one variable, the extent of association with delinquent friends, had a substantial effect on delinquent behavior. For 15-year-old boys, however, family and school variables also affected delinquent behavior, sometimes more than association with delinquent friends. Although their sample size was small, and the age-specific subsamples were even smaller (81 to 138 cases for the three separate age groups), their study raises the important point that the results of multivariate causal analysis may vary, at least with regard to the strength of relationships, depending on the age of the respondents in the sample. Because their data are cross-sectional (different age groups measured in the same year), it is not possible to rule out another potential explanation: The differences may not be age specific, but may be cohort specific instead. Full resolution of this issue would require a replication, preferably with longitudinal data.

Using data from the National Youth Survey, a prospective longitudinal panel survey of respondents aged 11-17 in 1976 and 21-27 in 1986, Menard et al. (1989) found that marriage during adolescence was positively associated with substance use and mental health problems, but that marriage during young adulthood (ages 21-27) was negatively associated with substance use and mental health problems. Being enrolled in school had a negative association with illegal behavior, substance use, and mental health problems in adolescence, but no association with illegal behavior, substance use, or mental health problems for young adults. Wofford (1989), analyzing the same sample, found that employment was associated with higher rates of serious illegal behavior in adolescence and lower rates of serious illegal behavior in young adulthood (ages 18-24 in this study). Substantively, these results require explanation. It may be that there exist age-specific norms for certain behaviors (school, marriage, work), and that violating those norms places one at greater risk of involvement in illegal or problem behavior. Methodologically, these results suggest that relationships among variables may change over the course of the life cycle, and that it may be appropriate to test for the existence of such changes. With cross-sectional data, such differences may be attributed to age or to intercohort differences; with longitudinal data on multiple cohorts, it becomes possible to estimate the extent to which the differences are developmental, as opposed to period or intercohort differences.

Causal Relationships

In order to establish the existence of a causal relationship between any pair of variables, three criteria are essential (Asher, 1976; Baltes and Nesselroade, 1979: 35; Blalock, 1964; Williamson et al., 1982: 218-219): (1) the phenomena or variables in question must covary, as indicated for example by differences between experimental and control groups or by a nonzero correlation between the two variables; (2) the relationship must not be attributable to any other variable or set of variables, i.e., it must not be *spurious,* but must persist even when other variables are controlled, as indicated for example by successful randomization in an experimental design (no differences between experimental and control groups prior to treatment) or by a nonzero partial correlation between two variables with other variables held constant; and (3) the supposed cause must precede or be simultaneous with the supposed effect in time, as indicated by the change in the cause occurring no later than the associated change in the effect.[2] Evidence for the first two criteria may be obtained from purely cross-sectional or time-ordered cross-sectional data. The third criterion can usually be tested adequately only with longitudinal data. One exception is if biological or genetic characteristics (sex, race) are among the variables thought to produce an effect. With such variables, we may safely assume temporal order without longitudinal data because, in effect, whenever a fixed or heritable trait is suggested as a cause of a variable characteristic (political attitudes, illegal behavior), we have data that are at least partially time ordered; we know that the fixed trait must have occurred first. Put another way, the measurement of fixed biological or genetic characteristics may be made *at* a particular period, but it is *for all* periods, beginning at birth.

The situation becomes more complex if there is a possibility of a *nonrecursive* causal relationship. In some theories, causal influences flow not only from X to Y, but from Y to X as well. For example, Malthus (Appleman, 1976) hypothesized that (a) increased food supply per capita leads to increased fertility, and (b) increased fertility leads to decreased food supply per capita. With only cross-sectional data, issues of causal order or direction regarding bivariate relationships cannot be resolved without agreement *a priori* on the elimination of causal relationships in certain directions (Blalock, 1962; Heise, 1975; Simon, 1954). Where there is a nonrecursive causal pattern involving a negative feedback loop, as suggested in Malthusian theory (above), it becomes extremely difficult to adequately model the process with only cross-sectional data, even using two- or three-stage least-squares or other fairly sophisticated methods of data analysis. With longitudinal panel data (repeated cross-sectional data may not be adequate here) it becomes more likely that the issues of causal order can be resolved, and that tests for causal influences in both directions can be made. (It is more probable, but not logically guaranteed, that longitudinal data will permit reliable estimates of reciprocal effects; for example, measurement periods may not be precise enough to separate the occurrence of changes in one variable from the occurrence of changes in another, and thus to resolve the issue of indeterminate ordering.) In the example of Malthusian theory, with its negative feedback loop, fairly long time-series data may be required for an adequate test of the theory.

One approach to identifying causal direction that allows for the identification of reciprocal causal influences is linear panel analysis, discussed extensively by Kessler and Greenberg (1981). Menard (1990) used linear panel analysis to test for reciprocal effects in the context of competing theories of the relationships among fertility, mortality, family planning program effort, and economic development. A series of models were calculated with each variable in turn considered as a dependent variable, and all variables, measured at a time prior to the measurement of the dependent variable (including a lagged endogenous variable, i.e., the dependent variable measured at a previous time) are included as predictors of the dependent variable. Within this framework, the possibility that each variable has some effect on each other variable may be examined in a way that is impossible with cross-sectional data. The inclusion of a lagged endogenous variable in the equation helps control for effects of unmeasured variables and provides a relatively conservative test for the existence of a (nonzero) causal relationship. Menard found evidence for reciprocal causal relationships not included in previous cross-sectional models of fertility, and also found evidence that the supposed causal order used in previous studies may have been incorrect (i.e., the models may have been misspecified).

Such findings are particularly useful because they deal with relationships among variables that tend to change continuously and for which ascertaining true temporal order may be difficult (e.g., a nation does not "initiate" fertility or economic development at some identifiable time; both occur continuously throughout the existence of the nation, and one cannot say that one "started" before the other). Note that the reciprocal effects identified in this type of analysis are not instantaneous, but lagged over time. Each of the models (estimated for each dependent variable) is technically recursive, because there are no "instantaneous" reciprocal effects; it is only by combining the results of the models for each of the separate dependent variables that we can infer the existence of bidirectional or nonrecursive causal influences.

True Temporal Order and Causal Relationships. In some cases, it may be possible to identify a distinct "start" for two variables, and to ascertain the true temporal order between the two. In such cases, one cannot necessarily infer that the first variable to change causes the second (the criteria of covariation and nonspuriousness must still be met), but such a test would provide evidence that the second variable to change did *not* cause the first. Elliott et al. (1989) and Huizinga et al. (1989) examined the relationship between illegal behavior and drug use, and concluded that if one causes the other, it is more likely that illegal behavior leads to drug use than that drug use leads to illegal behavior. *All* respondents who ever became involved in both illegal behavior (excluding alcohol, marijuana, and hard drug use) and alcohol use became involved in illegal behavior first; *all* of those who ever became involved in both illegal behavior and marijuana use became involved in illegal behavior first; and *all* of those who ever became involved in both illegal behavior and hard drug use became involved in illegal behavior first. If a cause must precede an effect in time, then the onset of alcohol and drug use are largely ruled out as causes of the onset of illegal behavior. The most plausible conclusions would be either that illegal behavior causes alcohol and drug use, or that illegal behavior and drug use have common causes (i.e., the relationship is spurious), and illegal behavior tends to occur before alcohol or drug use as a result of these causes. Based on evidence in Elliott et al. (1985, 1989), the latter explanation (spurious relationship) appears more likely. In a related study, Menard and Elliott (1990a) tested two theories: One suggested that involvement with delinquent friends leads to delinquent behavior, and the other suggested that delinquent behavior leads to involvement with delinquent friends. They found that association with delinquent friends typically preceded a respondent's own involvement in delinquent behavior, thus indicating support for the first theory (learning theory) and evidence against the second (control theory). Again, the establishment of temporal order is not in itself sufficient to establish causality, but it does provide evidence of the plausibility of one causal relationship as opposed to another.

Other Issues in Causal Analysis. In addition to addressing issues of causal order and the existence of reciprocal effects, longitudinal data and analysis in conjunction with causal modeling may be used to examine the distinction between long- and short-term effects on behavior. McCord (1983) found long-term consequences on adult aggression and antisocial behavior of childhood aggressiveness, parental aggressiveness, parental control, and parental affection. Studies of the Perry Preschool Project (Berrueta-Clement et al., 1984; Schweinhart and Weikart, 1980; Weikart et al., 1978), a Head Start-type preschool program, found short-term effects on student behavior and learning that seemed to dissipate in later years, then reemerge as long-term effects as the students entered adolescence. With methods such as event history analysis (Allison, 1984), it becomes easier, given appropriate data, to directly combine the analysis of age and period effects with causal analysis to explain developmental and historical change. These examples fall under the broader headings of describing change and of causal analysis, yet they indicate that questions about change and causality may sometimes be more complex (long- vs. short-term change; causal influences on rates of change) than simple questions of whether and why changes occur. The type of question that is asked may have important implications for which of several possible longitudinal designs is most appropriate for a particular study.

Serendipity and Intentionality in Longitudinal Data

The earliest longitudinal data in the social sciences, national census data, were probably not originally collected for the purposes of measuring change or of establishing the direction or magnitude of causal relationships. More typically, the two purposes of early censuses were conscription and taxation (Thomlinson, 1976). Later, in the United States, political apportionment was the only constitutionally mandated purpose of the census, and in more recent years the census has also been used as a basis for allocating funds from the federal government to the states. The fact that census data may be used to measure change and perhaps to infer the nature of causal relationships has been, at least until recently, more serendipitous than intentional. The same may be said about many other sources of longitudinal data as well. In the twentieth century, and especially since World War II, the collection of longitudinal data for the analysis of change and causality has become more conscious and deliberate, as social science research generally, and longitudinal research in particular, have come to be more highly valued by governments and by the scientific community. Still, it remains the case that longitudinal research is a secondary, not primary, reason for the collection of much periodic data by government agencies. As a result, methods of collecting data or definitions of variables may change in ways that render data less than fully comparable from one period to another.

In demography, for example, the United Nations has attempted to set standards for the counting of infant deaths and the calculation of infant mortality rates. Aside from problems of cross-national standardization, the adoption of those standards by countries such as Sweden in 1960 and Spain in 1975 (Hartford, 1984) produced discontinuities in the data so that comparisons of infant mortality rates over certain time periods, e.g. from 1970 to 1980 in Spain, are imprecise and problematic. Completeness of registration or counting of events may also vary over time, again making even crude measurements of change problematic. The President's Commission on Law Enforcement and the Administration of Justice (1967) cautioned that problems in coverage of rural areas in the United States rendered the crime statistics reported by the Federal Bureau of Investigation (annual) prior to 1958 "neither fully compatible with nor nearly so reliable" as data reported for subsequent years. Issues such as these may be more adequately addressed when data are collected primarily for longitudinal research to begin with, but it is worth cautioning that data that are initially collected for other purposes, and to which researchers serendipitously have access, should be carefully scrutinized to determine their suitability for the purposes of longitudinal research. Changes in how units or events are defined and counted, or in the extent to which the intended universe of cases is adequately sampled, may render some data sets unsuitable for use in longitudinal research.

3. DESIGNS FOR LONGITUDINAL DATA COLLECTION

Not-Quite-Longitudinal Designs

In Chapter 1, longitudinal research was contrasted with pure cross-sectional research, in which data are collected only once, contemporaneously, for each variable for each case. Prospective panel, retrospective panel, and repeated cross-sectional designs were described. Some studies do not fall neatly under the definition of longitudinal research or of pure cross-sectional research. Ahluwalia (1974, 1976) used data on per capita gross national product and income inequality to examine the relationship between income inequality and economic development. Because data on income inequality are collected sporadically, Ahluwalia used data in which, for each case, income inequality and per capita gross national product were measured at the same time, but for different countries (cases) measurement occurred in different years (e.g., for one country the two variables would be measured for the year 1955, and for another country the two variables would be measured for the year 1972). By performing a single, cross-sectional analysis on data collected over an 18-year span (1965-1972), Ahluwalia's analysis implicitly assumed that the 18 years constituted a single period. Equivalently, this approach assumed that the data on both per capita gross national product and income inequality were stable (no major changes in values, or at least in the ranking, of countries on these variables), or at least that the relationship between these variables remained largely unchanged over this 18-year time span. Such an assumption should be made only after careful consideration, and preferably with empirical support as well. Contrary to the assumption of stability, Menard (1983, 1986) presented evidence of instability in income inequality over time, to the point that for the period included in Ahluwalia's data, the ranking of countries with respect to income inequality changed. At the same time, per capita gross national product remained stable. In effect, Ahluwalia's data may represent a series of cross-sections in which the same variables are measured repeatedly, but the cases are neither comparable nor identical from one period to the next. The period used is so long that there is reason to doubt that the measurements for all of the cases could properly be considered contemporaneous.

In a somewhat different vein, Tolnay and Christenson (1984) deliberately selected variables that were measured at different times for use in a causal path analysis of fertility, family planning, and development. Each variable was measured at the same time for all countries, but different variables were measured at different times, in order to match the temporal order of measurement with causal order in the path model. This is just the opposite of the pattern in Ahluwalia's data. For Ahluwalia, variables are measured at the same time for each case, but cases are measured at different times; for Tolnay and Christenson, cases are measured at the same time for each variable, but variables are measured at different times. Although measurement occurs at different times for different variables, each variable is measured only once for each case, and the data cannot be used to perform even the simplest true longitudinal analysis (e.g., measuring change in a variable from one period to another). The analysis used by Tolnay and Christenson is essentially cross-sectional in nature. Had they chosen to postulate instantaneous effects, the analysis could have been performed just as well with purely cross-sectional data. For the purposes of their analysis (evaluating direct and indirect effects of family planning effort and development on fertility), this design is appropriate, and may have an advantage over models in which causal order in the path model and temporal order of measurement are not the same (Menard and Elliott, 1990a). The design used by Tolnay and Christenson, with time-ordered data and cross-sectional analysis, may be described as a *time-ordered cross-sectional design*. Although it is not truly a longitudinal design by the definition presented earlier, it may have some advantages over a pure cross-sectional design for purposes of causal analysis.

The use of time-ordered cross-sectional data, as in Tolnay and Christenson (1984), is desirable once temporal order has been established, but it is insufficient to ensure that one does not "predict" a cause from its effect. Suppose, for example, that the true causal relationship between two variables, X and Y, is the relationship diagrammed in Figure 3.1. Prior values of X influence subsequent values of X; prior values of Y influence subsequent values of Y; and prior values of Y influence subsequent values of X — that is, Y is a cause of the effect X with some finite time lag. Suppose, however, that we mistakenly believe X to be a cause of Y, and in a time-ordered cross-sectional design, we include X_2 as a cause of Y_3, excluding all other X (X_1 and X_3) and Y (Y_1 and Y_2). Despite the fact that we have the wrong causal order, we will probably discover a relationship between X_2 and Y_3, if only because X_2 is directly affected by Y_1 and Y_3 is indirectly (via Y_2) influenced by Y_1. If the variables change relatively slowly over time (i.e., if they are relatively stable), then similar correlations will be obtained whether we compare X_2 and Y_3, X_3 and Y_2, or some purely cross-sectional combination (e.g., X_2 and Y_2) of the two variables. With a true longitudinal design (e.g., a prospective panel design) and analysis, it might be possible to ascertain the true causal

24

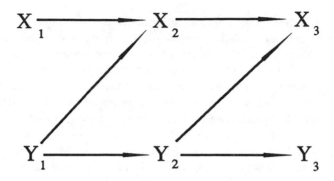

Figure 3.1. Hypothetical Causal Relationship between X and Y.

direction in the relationship between X and Y. Two-wave linear panel analysis with lagged endogenous variables should, in principle, be able to detect the fact that Y influences X but X does not influence Y (e.g., Menard, 1990). With cross-sectional data, even time-ordered cross-sectional data, one runs the risk of undetectable misspecification because of incorrect causal ordering in the model being estimated. With longitudinal data, incorrect causal ordering is more likely to be detected, e.g., by temporal order analysis or panel analysis, and the model may be corrected.

Total Population Designs

Figure 3.2 represents four types of longitudinal designs. In Figure 3.2, the horizontal dimension represents the period (a month, year, or decade) for which data are collected, and the vertical dimension represents the cases (population or sample) for which data are collected. In a *total population design*, the total population is surveyed or measured in each period of the study. Because some individuals die and others are born from one period to the next, the cases are not identical from one period to the next, but if the periods are short, the overwhelming majority of cases may be the same from one period to the next. As one example, the decennial census of the United States attempts to collect data on age, sex, ethnicity, and residence of the total population of the United States every 10 years, and does so with an accuracy estimated at 95-99% (Robey, 1989). With somewhat lower, but still substantial accuracy and completeness of coverage, the Federal Bureau of Investigation's *Uniform Crime Reports* attempt to collect data on arrests for specific offenses and, for a limited set of offenses, crimes known to the police,

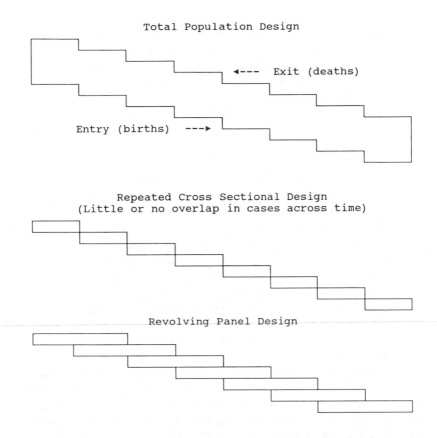

Figure 3.2. Longitudinal Designs for Data Collection.

and the age, sex, race, and residence (urban, suburban, or rural) of arrestees for all police jurisdictions in the United States.

As with any data-collection effort, the total population design may have problems of missing cases or measurement error. Because the total population is included, the design should be appropriate for measuring or inferring period trends, but close examination of age and cohort effects (as discussed earlier) may be necessary to clarify the nature of those trends. For example, apparent changes in the number or rate of arrests may reflect changes in population composition (percent in the arrest-prone adolescent ages) rather than changes in individual or group behavior (Chilton and Spielberger, 1971). Separation of age, period, and cohort effects is thus as much an issue for the total population design as for any other design, but the design poses no special problems in this regard. Developmental changes may be examined both cross-sectionally (within a given year, across cohorts) and longitudinally (within a given cohort across years, if there are enough periods to examine the developmental change in question), and the results of the two approaches for evaluating developmental effects may be compared. With proper selection of appropriate periods, cohorts, or other subpopulations, any type of longitudinal analysis may be performed on data collected in a total population design, again with the qualification that there are enough separate periods to permit use of a particular method. For example, linear panel analysis typically requires only two or three periods (Kessler and Greenberg, 1981), but ARIMA time-series models ideally involve a minimum of 50 observations in 50 distinct periods (Box and Jenkins, 1970: 18; McCleary and Hay, 1980: 20).

Each of the other three longitudinal designs in Figure 3.2 involves a sample drawn from the total population, and is thus a subset of the total population design. The three designs differ in the extent to which the same or comparable cases are studied from one period to the next. This distinction has important implications for which types of longitudinal analysis are possible with each design.

Repeated Cross-Sectional Designs

In the repeated cross-sectional design, the researcher typically draws independent probability samples at each measurement period. These samples will typically contain entirely different sets of cases for each period, or the overlap will be so small as to be considered negligible, but the cases should be as comparable from one period to another as would be the case in a total population design. An example of the repeated cross-sectional design is the National Survey of Youth, conducted by Martin Gold and his associates (Gold and Reimer, 1975; Williams and Gold, 1972). Gold and his associates collected data on two separate national probability samples of youth, one in

1967 and one in 1972. From these samples, they were able to infer that despite changes in arrest rates of juveniles from 1967 to 1972, there was little actual change in self-reported delinquent behavior from 1967 to 1972. Johnston et al. (annual) have collected data on national probability samples of high school seniors since 1975. Their repeated cross-sectional data, like the data collected by Gold and his associates, permit the examination of trends in attitudes and behaviors within a specific age group over time. (Longitudinal prospective panel data are also available from the Monitoring the Future study for a subsample of those who were originally sampled as high school seniors.)

The principal limitations to the repeated cross-sectional design are its inappropriateness for studying developmental patterns within cohorts and its inability to resolve issues of causal order. Both of these limitations result directly from the fact that in the repeated cross-sectional design, the same cases are not measured repeatedly or for multiple periods. Developmental patterns may be examined by looking at differences across ages (i.e., across cohorts) for each measurement period in which multiple cohorts are measured, but the only advantage of the repeated cross-sectional design over a pure cross-sectional design for this purpose is that the repeated cross-sectional design builds in the possibility of replicating cross-sectional results across periods. This reduces, but does not eliminate, the possibility that the developmental patterns suggested by intercohort comparisons may not reflect the developmental patterns indicated by intracohort comparisons. For causal order, the absence of data on the same cases for two or more times means that temporal order analysis and linear panel analysis are not possible (unless — and this is quite unlikely — an adequate procedure for matching different cases measured in different periods is available). The measurement of change in repeated cross-sectional designs can be made only at the aggregate level, for the sample or for subsamples (e.g., males and females, ethnic groups, social classes). It cannot be made at the level of individual cases. Limitations such as these have led many authors, particularly in developmental psychology (e.g., Baltes and Nesselroade, 1979) to argue that the repeated cross-sectional design should not really be considered a longitudinal design. Baltes et al. (1979) nonetheless consider the repeated cross-sectional design (which they describe as a cross-sectional sequence) in the study of cohort effects.

The repeated cross-sectional design is generally appropriate for measuring aggregate period trends. *If* causal order is already well established, and *if* the time lag between cause and effect can be assumed to be short relative to the interval between measurement periods, the repeated cross-sectional design may also be used for causal analysis in models that are essentially cross-sectional in nature. *If* intercohort and intracohort developmental differences closely reflect one another, there is no obstacle to the use of the repeated cross-sectional design with multiple cohorts for the analysis of developmental patterns, again in an essentially cross-sectional analysis. For both causal inference and developmental analysis, other types of longitudinal designs are needed to indicate whether a repeated cross-sectional design may reasonably be used. Finally, the repeated cross-sectional design permits the researcher to replicate cross-sectional results from one period to another. If, however, we are interested in intracohort developmental changes, or in ascertaining causal order, other longitudinal designs for data collection are preferable.

Revolving Panel Designs

Revolving panel designs collect data on a sample of cases either retrospectively or prospectively for some sequence of measurement periods, then drop some subjects and replace them with new subjects. The revolving panel design may reduce problems of panel mortality and repeated measurement in prospective studies (to be discussed below), or problems of extended recall periods in retrospective studies. Retention of a particular set of cases over several measurement periods allows short-term measurement of change on the individual or case level, short-term analysis of intracohort developmental change, and panel analysis. Replacement of the subsample that is dropped in a measurement period with a new but comparable subsample of cases permits analysis of long-term patterns of aggregate change. If the time lag between cause and effect is smaller than the time (periods) for which cases are retained in the sample, analysis of temporal and causal order is possible. The combination of longitudinal data involving repeated measurement on some cases with data that do not involve repeated measurement on others may permit comparisons that can indicate whether repeated measurement is producing any bias in the data (e.g., increased or decreased willingness to report events after either building up some level of trust or finding out that reporting leads to long and tedious follow-up questions).

The National Crime Survey, funded by the Department of Justice and implemented by the U.S. Census Bureau, is a good example of a revolving panel design. Household members are periodically interviewed about criminal victimization of household members for seven offenses (rape, robbery, aggravated assault, simple assault, burglary, larceny, and motor vehicle theft). Households are selected for inclusion by probability sampling, interviewed seven times (at six-month intervals) over a three-year time span, then dropped from the sample and replaced by newly selected households. With the household as the unit of analysis, this permits analysis of both short-term trends in rates of victimization within households, and both short- and long-term trends in aggregate or average rates of victimization. Longer-term developmental trends within households, however, cannot be analyzed.

The Kansas City Police patrol experiment (Kelling et al., 1974) also used a revolving panel design to collect data on victimization. A sample of 1,200 households was used in the pretest, and half of the households were retained and the other half replaced for the posttest. As a result, it was possible to compare those who had been interviewed twice (pretest and posttest) with those who had been interviewed only once (posttest only) and to rule out the possibility that the results (no difference between control and experimental police beats) were a consequence of bias from repeated interviewing. The revolving panel design would also be appropriate for longitudinal research on individuals within a particular age range, such as adolescents or those over age 65, in order to prevent serious problems of sample attrition as respondents "age out" of adolescence or die in old age. The revolving sample for limited age ranges permits the researcher to maintain a sufficient number of cases (see, e.g., Kraemer and Thiemann, 1987) for complex analyses of small subsamples within the larger sample.

Longitudinal Panel Designs

In a longitudinal panel design, the same set of cases is used in each period. In practice, there may be some variation from one period to another as a result of missing data. For example, when cases are individuals, some of those individuals may die between one measurement and the next, others may not agree to cooperate, and others may move to new locations and not be found by the researcher. All of these are sources of *panel attrition,* and apply primarily to *prospective* panel designs, in which measurement or data collection occurs during more than one period. Panel attrition, as such, is not a problem for *retrospective* panel designs, in which data collection may occur only once, at one period, but in which data are collected for two or more periods (prior to or during the period in which the data are being collected). In retrospective panel designs, however, there may be sampling bias as a result of excluding respondents who have died by the last period for which the data are collected, or from whom data would otherwise have been available for earlier periods but not for the last period. In both retrospective and prospective panel designs, missing data may result from failure of the respondent to remember past events, behaviors, or attitudes, or from unwillingness by the respondent to divulge some information, and also from inability of the researcher to locate or obtain cooperation from some respondents. In principle, there need be no difference in the quality of the data obtained in prospective and retrospective panel designs, but differences do occur in practice (as discussed in Chapter 4).

A longitudinal panel design that includes multiple cohorts (as illustrated in Figure 3.2) should permit any type of longitudinal analysis, if the numbers of periods and cohorts are sufficient. Single cohort panel designs do not permit comparisons between cohorts, but multiple cohort designs permit analysis of age, period, and cohort effects; descriptions of developmental and historical change; analysis of the temporal order of events; linear panel analysis; and causal analysis. As an example, the National Youth Survey, conducted by Delbert S. Elliott and his associates (Elliott et al., 1983, 1985, 1989) selected a national probability sample of youth aged 11-17 (seven cohorts) in 1976 and has continued to reinterview this same sample periodically, most recently in 1990. Data from the National Youth Survey have been used to estimate and analyze period trends in illegal behavior (Menard, 1987a), to separate age, period, and cohort effects in drug use (Elliott et al., 1989; Menard and Huizinga, 1989) and illegal behavior (Elliott et al., 1989; Menard and Elliott, 1990b), to test and replicate a theoretical model of illegal behavior in adolescence and young adulthood (Elliott et al., 1985, 1989), and to ascertain the temporal order of variables in order to resolve contradictory claims by competing theories (Menard and Elliott, 1990a). These examples illustrate the breadth of analysis and results possible with multiple cohort prospective panel data.

Other Variations

The designs diagrammed in Figure 3.2 are not the only possible designs for longitudinal research. It is possible, for example, to have a revolving sample in which subsamples may be dropped for one period, then reincluded in the sample in a subsequent period. It is also possible to have a panel design in which cases are dropped, without replacement, after they meet some criterion (e.g., age 21). This latter design would result in a monotonically decreasing sample size that could pose problems for analysis of data from later years of the study. The general considerations associated with the various designs for data collection do not change, however, with modifications of the four designs presented in Figure 3.2, and variations on these basic designs must be evaluated in terms of their adequacy for describing short- and long-term historical trends (period effects); describing intercohort and intracohort developmental changes (age effects); separating age, period, and cohort effects; and ascertaining not only the strength but also the direction (e.g., by temporal order analysis or linear panel analysis) of causal influences. Total population designs and longitudinal panel designs can be used for practically any type of longitudinal analysis, given a sufficient number of cohorts and measurement periods. Other designs are more limited, and their appropriateness must be judged in the context of a particular research problem.

With each of these designs, the number of cases and periods may vary, and as a result of this variation, different methods of analysis may be appropriate. If both the number of cases and the number of periods are large (e.g., several thousand cases and 100 or more periods), the possibilities for analysis are limited only by the quality of the data. If the cases and periods are both few in number (e.g., 1-10 cases over 2-10 periods), then any quantitative analysis may be problematic.[3] More characteristically, the number of cases may be fairly large (e.g., 1,000 cases at the individual level, or 50 cases at the aggregate level) and the number of periods may be small (2-4), a situation for which linear panel analysis (Kessler and Greenberg, 1981) is one appropriate method. Alternatively, the number of cases may be small (1-10) and the number of periods may be large (50 or more), a condition most amenable to time-series analysis (McCleary and Hay, 1980; Wei, 1990). The number of cases is in principle independent of the type of design. In a total population design, for example, at the individual level, the total population of a tribal society may number fewer than 100. In aggregate analysis, a cohort or a population, rather than its individual members, may be the unit of analysis, and the number of these aggregate units may be small. At the other end of the continuum, the revolving sample in the National Crime Survey includes more than 100,000 individuals from 60,000 households. All of these possible combinations of type of design and number of cases are included within the broad category of longitudinal research.

4. ISSUES IN LONGITUDINAL RESEARCH

There is nothing unique about the methods used to collect data for longitudinal research. Longitudinal research, like cross-sectional research, relies upon three fundamental methods of gathering data: asking people questions, observing people's behavior, and observing the physical traces or results of people's behavior. Data may be collected for a single case, a small number of cases, or a very large number of cases; for everyone in a society, for a probability sample of people in a society, or for particular individuals who may or may not reflect either the society as a whole or some segment of society. Data may be kept and coded at the level of individuals or aggregated into households, census tracts, or nations. Periods for which data are collected may be short, consisting of a few hours, or long, consisting of several years. Standardized data-collection instruments may be used, or data collection may be an interactive process that is unique to each case. Both longitudinal and cross-sectional research may involve case studies, ethnographies, experiments, sample surveys, censuses, or archival data collection. The one principal distinction between longitudinal and cross-sectional data collection, as noted earlier, is that in longitudinal research, data are collected on each variable for at least two periods.

The problems that arise regarding data quality in cross-sectional research thus arise in similar fashion for longitudinal research. Problems of internal and external measurement validity; measurement reliability; sampling; appropriateness of questions to the population being studied; adequacy of the randomization procedures in experimental designs; effects of interaction between subjects or respondents and experimenters, interviewers, or observers (in microsocial data collection); issues of the relevance of the research (do we measure what is important or just what is easily measurable?); and research costs are as important in longitudinal research as they are in cross-sectional research. Some of these issues are even more problematic for longitudinal than for cross-sectional research. For example, biases in sampling may be amplified by repetition in repeated cross-sectional designs, or effects of researchers on respondents may be amplified by repeated contact between researchers and subjects in prospective panel designs. General discussions of these issues are available elsewhere (e.g., Babbie, 1989; Bailey, 1987; Williamson et al., 1982). Here, the focus is on issues and problems that are characteristic of longitudinal rather than cross-sectional designs.

Genesis Versus Prediction

Zazzo (1967) argued that a distinction should be made between the study of the *genesis* of behavior and the study of the *prediction* of behavior. Prediction, according to Zazzo, is concerned with the stability of population characteristics over time and the extent to which external influences (changes in environment, therapeutic intervention) may modify those characteristics. Genesis, by contrast, focuses on stages or sequences of qualitative changes, with the goal of discovering laws of growth or developmental change. According to Zazzo, the study of the genesis of behavior may require the use of more qualitative methods: discarding large samples and predefined hypotheses and variables in favor of intensive study of a small number of cases, initially with no hypotheses about what variables are important, and discarding age (and chronological time) as a continuum along which change is measured in favor of measuring change with respect to prior states. Zazzo cited the work of Piaget (see, e.g., Piaget 1948, 1951, 1952) as an example of research on genesis.

Without denying that the focus of most longitudinal research has been on prediction, rather than genesis (as defined by Zazzo), we may nonetheless note that research on genesis has not been neglected at either the macrosocial or the microsocial level. At the macrosocial level, Rostow (1960) proposed a theory of stages of economic development, Black (1966) attempted to define stages of political development or political modernization, and the theory of the demographic transition, in its various incarnations (e.g., Caldwell, 1976; Davis, 1963; Notestein, 1945; Thompson, 1929), although not without its critics (Van de Walle and Knodel, 1980), has proven to be a durable perspective, and a source for a great deal of research in demography (see, e.g., Menard, 1990; Tolnay and Christenson, 1984). At the microsocial level, Kandel and her associates (Kandel, 1975; Kandel and Faust, 1975; Kandel and Logan, 1984; Yamaguchi and Kandel, 1984a, 1984b) have examined the sequencing of stages of drug use, and found evidence of progression from alcohol to marijuana to other illicit drugs, with few moving to a more advanced stage without first entering an earlier (less serious) one. Kandel's work, which has been confirmed by other researchers (Huizinga et al., 1989), has also demonstrated that research on genesis of behavior need not be isolated from predictive research. She and her associates have not only described sequences of progression in drug use, but have also explained under what circumstances progression from one substance to another is most likely. To obtain a more complete account of patterns of development, then, we may study both the sequencing of behavior and the timing and correlates of progression from one stage to another.

Changes in Measurement Over Time

In 1930, Redfield (1930) published the results of his ethnographic study of a Mexican village, Tepoztlan, in which he described the village as harmonious and the people as well adjusted and content. Twenty-one years later, Lewis (1951) published his ethnographic study of the same village, and in contrast to Redfield, Lewis found considerable evidence of violence, cruelty, and conflict, both within the village and in its relationships with other villages (Gist and Fava, 1974: 513). Fifty-five years after Mead (1928) published her ethnographic findings from Samoa, Freeman (1983) questioned and contradicted Mead's findings with his own ethnographic evidence from Samoa. Because of the differences in time, it is unclear whether the differences in findings reflect true changes or merely different biases or orientations on the part of the observers.

The problems so vividly illustrated by discrepant ethnographic studies may also arise in survey research. Martin (1983) described unsuccessful attempts to replicate surveys of victimization and surveys of confidence in American institutions in repeated cross-sectional survey designs. With regard to victimization, an Urban Institute study explicitly designed to replicate the standard procedures used by the Census Bureau in conducting the National Crime Survey obtained victimization rates less than half those obtained for a comparable population in the National Crime Survey conducted one year later, and lower also than the rates obtained in a telephone survey conducted at about the same time. With regard to confidence in American institutions, nearly identical measures used by Harris polls and National Opinion Research Center studies produced not only different cross-sectional results, but different trends as well. In contrast, Gold's (Gold and Reimer, 1975; Williams and Gold, 1972) repeated cross-sectional study of delinquent behavior appears to have been successful in replicating both the sampling procedures and the substantive results from the first wave to the second.

One advantage to the surveys conducted by Gold and his associates was continuity with respect to the principal researcher. Without intimate knowledge of not only formal procedures, but informal aspects of the research as well, it may be extremely difficult or impossible to completely replicate previous waves of data collection in a repeated cross-sectional or prospective (total population, revolving panel, longitudinal panel) longitudinal designs. The problem of standardization across periods or waves of data collection may be different for different data-collection methods. Standardization across waves in survey research is aided by use of the same questionnaire from one wave of data to another, but variation in the way the questionnaire is administered by interviewers at different waves may still pose a problem; this is an issue, primarily, of interviewer training. For more qualitative research, the "instrument" for data collection may be the observer, and different observers may have different biases, focus on different aspects of the setting or behavior in the setting, and reach very different conclusions. Some researchers have suggested that the findings from participant observation studies may be inherently "idiosyncratic and difficult to replicate" (Blalock and Blalock, 1982: 97).

Lack of standardization in data collection across time may arise for legitimate reasons. If a survey begins with adolescent respondents and follows them until they are in their late twenties or early thirties, questions about how favorably they view school may be important in the early years of the survey, and questions about how favorably they view their job or occupation may be more important later. Respondents will also be making transitions from families of orientation (parents and siblings) to families of procreation (spouses and children). If attitudes toward work or school, and family stress, are theoretically important predictors of some behavior (e.g., drug use), it may make sense to match the changes in respondents' lives with corresponding changes in the variables that are measured. Two questions are important here. First, can one variable measured at one stage of a respondent's life be equated with a conceptually similar variable (e.g., stress in family of orientation and stress in family of procreation) at a later stage? Second, is the transition abrupt or gradual? Do respondents undergo a period when involvement in both contexts is important (e.g., working and going to school at the same time), or is the change an abrupt one that involves completely leaving one context and immersing oneself in the other? By measuring the variables for both contexts at the same time, it is possible to directly estimate the relationship between the two variables, and to see whether they have similar patterns of relationships with other variables. If the variables are highly correlated, and if they have the same pattern of relationships with other variables, a strong argument for concurrent validity (Williamson et al., 1982; Zeller and Carmines, 1980) may be established.

Other reasons for changes in instrumentation include new hypotheses, either from the study itself or from general advances in the relevant fields of social science, and changes in research staff and their respective interests (Wall and Williams, 1970). The addition of new hypotheses to those with which the study began may also be a source of change. The dangers involved with each of these changes are readily apparent. If other studies have clearly discredited or refuted the hypotheses upon which the research project is based, it becomes practically meaningless to continue the research. The utter refutation of a theory or hypothesis is, however, exceedingly rare in the social sciences, and even then, the data may have some utility for replicating the refutation of the old hypothesis. Alternatively, shifting hypotheses, variables, and measurements partway through an ongoing longitudinal research project would mean that the two parts of the research, before and after the shift, might not be comparable. This potentially destroys the utility of the data, both before and after the shift, for the sort of longitudinal analysis that was originally intended. In addition, it runs the risk of having one's research dictated by what may later be recognized as a transient theoretical fashion.

Panel Attrition

In a longitudinal study of adolescent drug use, Newcomb and Bentler (1988) experienced a 55% attrition rate over an eight-year interval. Murray and Erickson (1987) reported an attrition rate of 50% in a study of marijuana use. Other studies have fared better. The National Youth Survey (Elliott et al., 1989) reported an attrition rate of 13% over an eight-year time span. Clarridge et al. (1977) were able to achieve an attrition rate of 11% in a follow-up study of Wisconsin high school seniors 17 years after they were first interviewed. Other prospective longitudinal panels such as the Panel Study of Income Dynamics and the Survey of Income and Program Participation report retention rates (for those who responded in the first period of data collection) of 75-80% (Kalton et al., 1989).

Insofar as respondents are lost in later waves of data collection, the measurement of change may be confounded because those respondents who are lost may differ from those who are retained in some systematic way (they may have had different average values on variables to begin with, or they may have changed in ways different from the rest of the sample). This is especially serious if losses come disproportionately from those with extreme values on the variables on which the research focuses, for example, the most frequent illicit drug users or the most serious criminals in studies of illegal behavior. It is thus not only the magnitude of the attrition but also the pattern of attrition with respect to critical variables in the study that may be problematic.

Attrition rates will inevitably be high if the researcher fails to maintain contact with the research subjects. Burgess (1989) and Clarridge et al. (1977) discuss techniques of tracing respondents in some detail. These techniques include obtaining, on the first and subsequent interviews, names and addresses of parents, other relatives, friends, or other individuals with whom the respondent is likely to stay in touch, and repeated annual mailings (e.g., birthday cards or other special occasion greeting cards) with a request to the post office to supply a forwarding address if the respondent has moved. In order to maintain low attrition rates, substantial resources must be available for tracking respondents.

Clarridge et al. (1977), in a 17-year follow-up survey of more than 10,000 Wisconsin high school seniors, were able to locate 97.4% of the original respondents, and to obtain interviews from 88.6% of the original sample. Clarridge et al. used a variety of sources, beginning with parents and including colleges and high schools, the post office, military service, neighbors, and friends of the respondents to obtain their high response rates. Burgess (1989) concluded that it was reasonable in surveying most groups in the population to expect to contact or trace 80-90% of all respondents, even over extended time intervals between surveys. One may properly question whether the results of analyses of panel data with attrition rates of 50% or more can reasonably be generalized beyond the respondents who were retained in the study.

To some extent, the impact of panel attrition on the distribution of variables and the substantive findings for a data set may be ascertainable. The binomial test (Bulmer, 1979) may be used to test whether the proportion of individuals in different demographic categories (male or female, white or nonwhite, and so on) changes significantly over time. Other tests of statistical significance may be used to test whether, at the first wave of data collection, those who continued in later waves (stayers) differed from those who were later lost to the study (leavers) with respect to (a) values on particular variables, (b) strength of relationships (e.g., correlations) among variables, or (c) the structure of relationships (e.g., multiple regression equations or covariance structure) among sets of three or more variables. Such tests may uncover evidence of sample variability over successive waves of data collection. Still, it remains possible that some source of sample variability that significantly affects the substantive outcome of the analysis may be overlooked. For example, those with different behavioral trajectories (e.g., increasing as opposed to decreasing drug use) may be differentially likely to remain in or drop out of the panel, and this may not be readily detectable using the methods suggested above. This could seriously bias substantive results such as the estimation and explanation of developmental trends in behavior, and could be extremely difficult to detect.

In retrospective panel designs, the problem of attrition takes a different form, one not amenable to assessment by the use of tests of statistical significance. Instead of problems associated with respondents' leaving the panel after the first wave of data collection, retrospective studies may have problems of selection. Especially for long-term studies, retrospective studies may miss individuals who, for example, died or moved out of the area from which the sample was drawn, and who did so during the period for which the data were collected. Those individuals may differ systematically from the rest of the population. For example, frequent users of illicit drugs may have higher mortality than the rest of the population. If this is so, then frequent illicit drug users will be undersampled for the period of the study, and this may bias estimates of change in rates of illicit drug use. In effect, this is a problem of attrition, but attrition that takes place before the sample is drawn. It is much more difficult to detect and measure this type of attrition than the attrition that arises in conjunction with prospective panel designs.

Repeated Measurement and Panel Conditioning

The effect of panel conditioning (e.g., Kalton et al., 1989) in the continued study of a set of respondents is a problem primarily for microsocial, longitudinal panel designs, including experimental and quasi-experimental designs that involve a pretest. Effects of repeated testing may damage internal validity in experimental and quasi-experimental designs, but the use of control groups may allow the researcher to measure this effect and, if it is present, to determine whether there are treatment effects in addition to the changes resulting from repeated measurement. In one example drawn from survey research, the validity of the National Crime Survey appears to suffer from effects of repeated interviewing (Cantor, 1989). Mensch and Kandel (1988) found evidence of similar problems in a study of drug use conducted by the Center for Human Resource Research at The Ohio State University.

Willingness of respondents to answer questions in a way that will evoke a known response (e.g., follow-up questions) is only one threat to validity that emerges with the use of continued study of the same cases. More general unwillingness to participate in the study may also result from continued study and may result in attrition. Yet another possibility is that respondents will change as a result of participation in the survey. Since the introduction of a depression scale in the 1984 wave of the National Youth Survey, respondents who reported feeling depressed and having symptoms of depression according to a clinically based depression scale have had the option of requesting an anonymous referral to a mental health professional or facility. The simple fact of having this option may alter the attitudes or behavior of those respondents (who constitute a small proportion of the total sample). Collins et al. (1989) reported that in a study of family caregivers of elderly relatives, 52% identified at least one effect of study participation, most often involving how they (the caregivers) coped with the strains of providing in-home care for their elderly relatives. Rubin and Mitchell (1978) reported that couples in a longitudinal study of the development of relationships were also affected by the research. A common pattern seems to be for the respondents to be more aware of and introspective about their attitudes, emotions, and behavior. It is difficult to tell whether this, in turn, produces substantial changes in attitudes, emotions, or behavior. It is also unclear whether these effects would occur as the result of a single cross-sectional study, or whether they are peculiar to longitudinal research involving repeated contact between researchers and respondents.

It is not survey research alone that is susceptible to effects of continued study. Any prospective microsocial research, including observational research, in which there is contact between the researcher and the research subject or in which the subjects are aware that they are being observed risks this type of error. For macrosocial research, depending on how data are collected or accumulated, this may be less of a problem. The length of time for which the United States has been compiling official crime, census, and vital statistics data does not appear to have negatively affected the validity of those data over time. If anything, the opposite is the case. Census coverage has become increasingly complete over the duration of the U.S. Census, including the past several censuses (Robey, 1989), and thoroughness of coverage of police jurisdictions for the FBI Uniform Crime Reports has also increased over time. Similarly, international statistics on population, economic development, and other national characteristics do not appear to have gotten worse over time. Note, too, that retrospective studies may not be susceptible to the problem of continued study (although retrospective studies, like prospective and cross-sectional studies, may have problems if the interview process seems too long and tedious to the respondents).

The problem of continued study of a panel of subjects is thus primarily of concern for microsocial, prospective studies. Even for microsocial, prospective studies, it may be possible to avoid the problem, either by adjusting the interval between data-collection waves (the one- to three-year interval used in the National Youth Survey, as opposed to the six-month interval used in the National Crime Survey), by varying the design of the questionnaire from wave to wave (although that may raise another set of issues regarding the comparability of data from one wave of data collection to another), or by successfully encouraging a high level of commitment to the research on the part of subjects and research staff.

Respondent Recall

Sorenson et al. (1980) argued that retrospective designs provided accurate accounts of past delinquent behavior. To draw this inference, however, they relied on a comparison of cross-sectional surveys from two different populations (Contra Costa County, California, in 1965 and the St. Louis, Missouri, metropolitan area in 1981 and 1982). Based on the fact that the cross-sectional data for St. Louis in 1965 (collected retrospectively in 1981-1982) produced rates of illegal behavior similar to those found in the Contra Costa County data (collected prospectively) for 1965, they concluded that the retrospective data for St. Louis were valid. The defect of such an argument is that any similarity between the two may be a fortuitous combination of trends in the two areas that produce coincident rates in a particular period. In particular, if Contra Costa County had lower rates of illegal behavior in 1965 than St. Louis, and if the retrospective data for St. Louis underreported past illegal behavior, the two might agree on rates of illegal behavior despite problems in the validity of the retrospective data. A much better procedure would be to compare prospective and retrospective data from the same respondents.

Menard and Elliott (1990a) used data from the National Youth Survey to compare (a) trends in the prevalence of offending (the percentage of the respondents in the sample who reported having committed a particular offense) based on one-, two-, and three-year recall periods, and (b) the prevalence of serious offending based on prospective data with a one-year recall period and retrospective data with a variable recall period (typically 10 years). Comparisons of one-, two-, and three-year recall periods for general nondrug offending, serious (Index) nondrug offending, marijuana use, and other illicit drug use (polydrug use) are illustrated in Figure 4.1. The solid lines represent trends based on the prospective, one-year recall data for 1976-1983 (annual data were not available for 1981 and 1982; the solid lines simply connect the data points for 1980 and 1983). The dashed lines represent trends based on three-year recall data for 1981 and two-year recall data for 1982 (and connected to the data points for 1980 and 1983). For 1981-1983, the prospective data (based on 1980 and 1983) indicate stable or declining trends for general offending, Index offending, and marijuana use, but the extended recall data (for 1981 and 1982) indicate positive trends. For polydrug use, the extended recall data do not deviate a great deal from the one-year recall data, but for all four types of illegal behavior, there is a "dipper" effect, with trend lines based on long-term recall data dipping below the trend lines for the one-year recall data. Figure 4.1 is consistent with a pattern of increased forgetting as the interval over which the respondent is asked to remember events or behavior increases. The problem of memory decay appears less serious for some types of illegal behavior (hard drug use) than for others (general nondrug offending). Menard and Elliott considered other possible explanations of this pattern, but concluded that increased

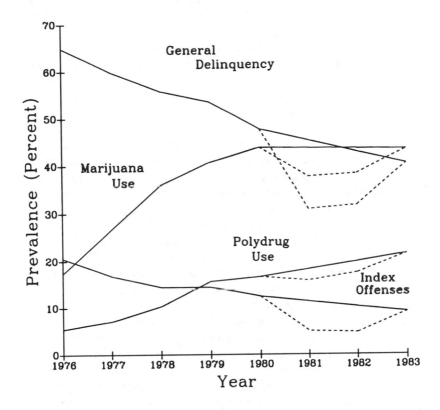

Figure 4.1. Period Trends Based on Long- and Short-Term Recall

memory decay with increasing length of the interval over which respondents are asked to remember events was the most plausible explanation for this pattern.

In the comparison of prospective (one-year recall) and retrospective (10-year recall) data, respondents were asked whether (and if so, when) they had ever committed each of several serious offenses (rape, robbery, aggravated assault, gang fighting, burglary, theft of more than $50, motor vehicle theft, and sale of hard drugs). Briefly, the prospective self-reports included more than 90% of the offenses reported on the retrospective self-reports, but the retrospective self-reports captured fewer than half of the offenses found by the prospective self-reports. These results are also consistent with the hypothesis of increasing memory decay for longer intervals. Other possible explanations for these patterns were examined by Menard and Elliott, but were again found to be less plausible than the explanation based on failure to remember events that occurred several years ago. Although these results do not rule out the use of retrospective data in general, it is clear that for some behaviors, long-term retrospective data are unreliable and may produce trends or effects opposite to those indicated by prospective data. Retrospective and prospective panel data should not be used interchangeably unless there is evidence that the extended recall period required by retrospective data does not result in underestimates of events in earlier years.

Issues of replication and recall may also include the phenomena of telescoping and reverse telescoping: reporting an event that happened in one period for a more or less recent period than the one in which it occurred. Evidence of telescoping has been found in the National Crime Survey (Lehnen and Skogan, 1981), and the first interview for National Crime Survey respondents is not used for estimating rates of victimization for the sample. Other studies attempt to use memory bounding techniques (e.g., reference to particular events such as birthdays or holidays) to reduce the impact of telescoping and reverse telescoping. The data from the National Youth Survey (Menard and Elliott, 1990a) also indicate some telescoping and reverse telescoping when retrospective and prospective data are compared.

Problems of respondent recall are problems primarily for microsocial interview research. The use of prospective panel designs helps to reduce these problems, but not to eliminate them altogether. Retrospective designs may have serious problems of validity because as the length of the time interval for which respondents are asked to report events or behavior increases, so does the likelihood of memory failure, memory reconstruction (Weis, 1986), and underreporting. For some purposes, such as measuring changes in attitudes over time, only prospective panel designs appear to be adequate. Finally, caution should be exercised when using repeated cross-sectional designs to measure change over time. Even relatively minor differences in sampling procedures or the administration of survey instruments may produce serious problems for replication, as Martin's (1983) examples indicate.

The Costs of Longitudinal Research

Wall and Williams (1970) suggested that the costs of prospective panel studies are probably no higher per wave of data collected than the costs of a similar number of cross-sectional studies. Six waves of a prospective longitudinal survey may cost no more than six cross-sectional studies with comparable populations and sample sizes. Although this may be true, it is important to consider whether one six-wave prospective longitudinal study is worth as much as or more than six separate cross-sectional studies, or worth six times as much as a retrospective panel study. Not all types of research require longitudinal data, and some that do could rely on secondary analysis of longitudinal data that had already been collected by other researchers.

For some purposes, longitudinal research is the only acceptable option. If the purpose is to measure historical or developmental change, a longitudinal design is essential, especially to separate age, period, and cohort effects. If change is to be measured over a long span of time, then a prospective panel design or total population design will usually be the most appropriate design for the research, because independent samples (in repeated cross-sectional designs) may differ from one another unless both formal and informal procedures for sampling and data collection are rigidly replicated for each wave of data (Martin, 1983). Also, recall failure may render inferences drawn from retrospective panel designs invalid. If change is to be measured over a relatively short time (weeks or months), then a retrospective design may be appropriate for data on events or behaviors, but probably not for attitudes or beliefs. Repeated cross-sectional designs or revolving panel designs may be appropriate if a problem of panel conditioning as a result of repeated interviewing or observation in a prospective panel is anticipated.

If the purpose of the research is to identify or estimate the strength of causal relationships, longitudinal research may again be preferable to cross-sectional research, especially if the true causal and temporal order of changes in variables is unknown. Hypotheses derived from theory, or worse, guesses about correct causal and temporal order are inadequate substitutes for knowledge about causal and temporal order, and temporal order is one aspect of a relationship that must be tested in order to determine whether a proposed causal relationship exists. The best tests of causal relationships involve the use of experimental designs (Babbie, 1989; Bailey, 1987; Campbell and Stanley, 1963; Williamson et al., 1982), and experimental designs are at least implicitly, and usually explicitly, prospective longitudinal designs.

If the measurement of change is not a concern, if causal and temporal order are known, or if there is no concern with causal relationships, then cross-sectional data and analysis may be sufficient. If, however, the research problem requires longitudinal data and analysis, it makes more sense to spend more money to get the right answer than to spend less money to get an inconclusive answer that may well be wrong. Under such circumstances, the question of whether longitudinal research is worth the cost does not really involve a question of whether longitudinal or cross-sectional methods should be used;

it involves a question of whether the cost of the longitudinal research is justified by the importance of the research problem that is being considered. The choice should be between doing the research properly, or not doing it at all.

5. LONGITUDINAL ANALYSIS

In Chapter 2, two primary purposes for longitudinal research were described: the description of patterns of change, and the analysis of causal relationships. This final chapter presents a broad overview of analytical methods for accomplishing these purposes. In so doing, it shifts from a focus on longitudinal *data collection* to a focus on longitudinal *data analysis,* what to do with the data once they are collected. The various methods for longitudinal data analysis are described in detail elsewhere, and it is not the purpose of this chapter to demonstrate how to use each method. Instead, the focus is on the different types of research questions that may be addressed by longitudinal research and the different methods that may be used to answer those questions. More detailed explication of the methods of longitudinal analysis may be found in the sources cited in connection with the respective methods.

Conceptualizing and Measuring Change

The most fundamental task for longitudinal research may also be the most difficult. First, a distinction needs to be made between qualitative and quantitative change. The measurement of qualitative change is straightforward: Either there is a change in the value of the variable (e.g., in qualitative states), or there is not. For example, one either moves from being a nondelinquent (no delinquent activity) to being a delinquent (some delinquent activity), or one remains a nondelinquent. One moves from being a blue-collar worker to being a white-collar worker, or one remains a blue-collar worker. For each separate category of each variable, the pattern is the same: One either changes or one does not. Measurement of purely qualitative change may thus involve a simple yes-no dichotomy. If categories are ordinal and few in number, the dichotomous measurement of change is adequate, but for ordinal scales with many categories a more detailed, quantitative measure of change may be feasible or desirable. More extensive specification of *how* a case has changed may be desirable (e.g., for the nominal scale "religion," we may want to know whether one converted from Protestantism to Roman Catholicism or to Judaism), but in principle this just means constructing a set of categories based on different dichotomous possibilities of change (one for each state at time 1 and one for each corresponding state at time 2). *Whether* there has been any change is still a dichotomous measure.

For continuous measurement scales, two measures of change are commonly considered. One is the *difference* between the later score and the earlier score on a variable as defined by subtraction: $X_2 - X_1$, where the subscripts refer to time periods. This may be called a difference, a *change score,* a *raw change,* or a *raw gain.* A second measure that has been used in research on change is the *residual gain.* In order to calculate a residual gain, the variable Y_2 is first regressed (using linear regression) on Y_1 in order to obtain a predicted or *expected* value for Y_2. The expected value of Y_2, $E(Y_2)$, depends on the value of Y_1 and the values of two parameters, a (the intercept; the expected value of Y_2 when Y_1 is zero) and b (the slope of the best fitting line for describing the relationship between Y_2 and Y_1): $E(Y_2) = a + bY_1$. The residual gain score is the difference between the actual value of Y_2 and the expected or predicted value of Y_2:

$$\text{Residual gain } (Y) = Y_2 - E(Y_2) = Y_2 - a - bY_1$$

For ratio scales, there is a third commonly used measure of change. The *percent change* in Z is: Percent change $(Z) = 100\%(Z_2 - Z_1)/Z_1$. Note that this measure is not appropriate for use with anything other than a ratio scale because for any scale without a nonarbitrary zero point, there exists an infinite number of different but equally valid measures of percent change. To illustrate this point, consider temperature as an example. On this interval scale, the percent change from room temperature to the boiling point of water is $100\%(212 - 70)/70 = 203\%$ for the Fahrenheit scale, but for the Celsius scale it is $100\%(100 - 21)/21 = 376\%$. Variations on this measure of change include the average annual percentage growth (or change), and measures based on rates other than percentages (e.g., rates per 1,000 or per 100,000). Another measure of change for ratio scales is the compound rate of change, the most familiar example of which is the compounding of interest in a savings account.

Any measure of change may be used over more than one unit of time. One simply divides the change by the number of periods (or other units of time, not necessarily equal in length to the periods used for measurement) over which the change occurs in order to obtain a raw gain, residual gain, or percent change per unit time. For descriptive purposes, the selection of one measure of quantitative change over another may be largely a matter of taste, except that residual gain scores should be used to identify those cases that, given some initial level or value on the variable whose change is being described, changed more or less than would be expected.

Measuring Change to Analyze Change. Measuring change for the purpose of analyzing, predicting, or explaining change (e.g., in a causal model) is more problematic than measuring change for descriptive purposes. There is some disagreement in the social and behavioral science literature about the appropriateness of raw gain scores as measures of change when the purpose is to analyze change. Cronbach and Furby (1970) argued against the use of raw gain scores because raw gain scores are systematically related to any random error of measurement,[4] are typically less reliable than the scores of the variables (e.g., X_1 and X_2) from which they are calculated, and the unreliability of raw gain scores may lead to fallacious conclusions or false inferences. They also argued against the use of residual gain scores as change variables (for similar reasons), and suggested that residual gain scores be used only (as a more appropriate alternative to gain scores for this purpose) to identify cases that changed more or less than expected based on their initial scores. Plewis (1985) concurred and observed that the problem of measurement error is just as serious for residual gain scores as for raw gain scores. As an alternative to models that use raw gain or residual gain scores, models with lagged endogenous variables have been suggested by these and other authors (Kessler and Greenberg, 1981).

A qualified dissent is offered by Liker et al. (1985). They demonstrate that *first difference equations* that involve the use of raw gain scores may be superior to both cross-sectional equations and the use of lagged endogenous variables for linear models in which (a) regression parameters remain constant from one period to another, (b) there are unmeasured variables that influence the dependent variable but do not change over time, (c) there is autocorrelated error in the measurement of those variables that both influence the dependent variable and vary over time, and (d) the panel data give more reliable measurement of *changes* in predictor variables over time than of the level or value of predictor variables at any given time. First difference equations are formed by taking two cross-sectional equations, one for time t and one for time $t + 1$, and subtracting the earlier from the later equation. All variables in the equation are then expressed as differences. Note that the conditions under which first difference equations are preferable to other methods of analysis are quite restrictive. The condition that change in a variable be measured more accurately than the level of a variable, in particular, almost begs the question raised by Cronbach and Furby (1970), who make the point that it is typically *not* the case that change in a variable is measured more reliably than level of a variable.

Baltes and Nesselroade (1979) suggested that "the problems so often cited within the context of measuring change seem to arise from uncertainty concerning how change should be defined and from the use of measurement and scaling procedures whose properties prompt little faith in the validity of derived measures, such as change scores." Plewis (1985) qualified his own reservations about difference scores by suggesting that they may be appropriate for some economic data, which he suggested might be measured more accurately than data in the other social sciences. Baltes and Nesselroade also observed that it may be impracticable to avoid altogether the use of difference scores, especially in applied research that uses a pretest-posttest design to estimate the effects of a treatment or intervention. The conclusion to be drawn from all of this is that the decision to use any sort of measure of change in an analysis of change is not a simple issue, and may depend on the theoretical justification for using a change measure (Cronbach and Furby suggested that such justification rarely exists), the reliability of change measures as compared with the reliability of measurement of the variables from which the change measures are derived, and the presumed specification of the relationship among the variables in the model (Liker et al., 1985).

Other Issues in the Measurement of Change. Any of the change measures described above may be used for either individual cases or for groups of cases (e.g., males and females; more developed and less developed countries) in total population designs, panel designs, and (for some cases over a limited span of time) revolving panel designs. In repeated cross-sectional designs, measurement of change for individual cases is not really possible, but change may be measured for well-defined groups of cases as long as the cases are comparable at the group level from one cross section to the next. For probability samples of the population with adequate numbers of cases in each group, this should pose little problem as long as sampling and the administration of the data collection are strictly replicated, but any deviation from the original sampling or administration procedures may seriously compromise the comparability of the data and may render the repeated cross-sectional data useless for longitudinal analysis (Martin, 1983). All of the longitudinal designs described in Figure 3.2 may be used to measure change for the full sample or population, but again with repeated cross-sectional designs care must be taken to be sure that the sampling and administrative procedures are the same for different cross sections.

Whenever we attempt to measure change, we need to consider whether apparent differences from one time to another really indicate change, or whether they may indicate unreliability of measurement instead. Previously cited examples illustrate this problem. Were the different conclusions of Redfield (1930) and Lewis (1951) in Tepoztlan, Mexico, the result of unreliability (one or both of the observers were biased and gave an inaccurate account of life in the village) or did the village change substantially in the time from Redfield's observation to the time when Lewis conducted his research? Does the negative association between number of times interviewed and number of victimization incidents reported in the National Crime Survey (Cantor, 1989) reflect unreliability in the National Crime Survey data, a real decline (possibly the result of a "treatment" effect in which responding to the survey provokes respondents to think about their victimization experiences more deeply, and to take precautions to avoid victimization), a sampling problem (are those with the highest rates of victimization disproportionately likely to change households and thus to leave the sample?), or a real period trend in victimization? The characteristics of the sample with respect to length of time in the sample presumably would have stabilized in 1976 (i.e., the number of respondents or households that had been interviewed once, twice, three times, and so forth would be expected to remain the same after the first three years because the sample revolves on a three-year cycle), and estimated victimization rates for most offenses have declined in the NCS panel since 1976 (U.S. Department of Justice, 1988, 1989). It is thus possible that some of the decline in victimization rates measured on repeated interviews is attributable to real period trends in victimization, but it is unlikely that period trends can explain all of the observed change (Cantor, 1989). Interestingly, it is possible that trends in victimization are measured more accurately than levels of victimization because since 1976 the National Crime Survey has probably had the same distribution of systematic error within the sample; if so, this would satisfy one of the conditions suggested by Liker et al. (1985) for use of first difference rather than lagged endogenous models to analyze victimization.

Recall that test-retest reliability measures (but not internal consistency reliability measures) are themselves measures of change when it is assumed that no change has actually occurred (Zeller and Carmines, 1980). The dilemma of separating unreliability of measurement from real change may best be addressed by replication and the use of multiple, independent measures of reliability and change. In some instances, other evidence may clearly favor one explanation (e.g., reliability) over the other (e.g., change). For example, changes in prevalence of illegal behavior may be similar across age groups in an age-specific analysis, and these changes may be independent of the number of previous interviews; this would suggest real change instead of unreliability. If changes varied across age groups in a way that appeared to be linked with the number of previous interviews, a stronger case could be made for unreliability.

Describing Patterns of Change

The description of a pattern of change may typically take one of three forms: numerical, graphical, or mathematical (including statistical). Numerical descriptions of change simply involve the presentation of the numerical value of some measure of change, for example, the annual percentage change in the per capita gross national product. Graphical descriptions of change generally involve plotting values of a variable for different periods on a graph on which time is the horizontal axis and the variable is on the vertical axis. Figure 4.1 is an example of a graphical depiction of change and indicates whether trends are upward, downward, or stable for any given time interval, and whether and how trends change over time.

Patterns of change in quantitative variables may be described mathematically by deterministic or probabilistic models. In deterministic models, change is conceptualized as following some fixed pattern or law. Knowing how the values of some relevant, finite set of predictor variables change for a specific case permits us to know with certainty whether the value of a predicted or dependent variable for that case will change, how it will change (increase or decrease), and by how much it will change. In practice, in the social sciences, there is likely to be some deviation from predictions of deterministic models, if only as a result of measurement error, but in principle we can know exactly whether, how, and by how much one variable changes in response to changes in other variables, for individual cases, groups (e.g., males and females or more and less developed countries), or for an entire sample or population of cases.

In probabilistic models, if we know how the values of some relevant, finite set of predictor variables change for the total population, the sample, or a group of sufficient size (males and females, more and less developed countries), we can predict with some accuracy the *proportion* or *percentage* of cases that will change, the proportion or percentage that will change in a certain way, and the *average* (mean, median, modal) amount by which they will change. (This is analogous to the situation in the physical sciences with quantum mechanics; see note 2.) This is because the underlying assumption in probabilistic models is that there is some influence or set of influences on behavior that, on the individual case level, operates as a probabilistic process. Cases with certain characteristics may be more or less likely than cases with other characteristics to change in a specified way, but individual cases need not be consistent in their patterns of change with other cases in the group or sample.

One way of viewing this pattern is to think of individuals as having various influences on their behavior (stronger influences in a particular direction for some individuals or groups, weaker influences for others), but at the same time as having some freedom to choose among different patterns of behavior, and even to resist strong influences in a particular direction. Some individuals will choose to resist the measurable influences on their behavior, even if those influences are strong, but a smaller percentage of cases will resist a strong influence than will resist a weak influence (implying a smaller error of prediction for a strong influence).

Univariate Models of Quantitative Change. Deterministic univariate models of change in quantitative variables in the social sciences include functional equations (Kim and Roush, 1980: 101-104), difference equations (Huckfeldt et al., 1982; Kim and Roush, 1980, Chapter 5), and differential equation models (Blalock, 1969: 88-91; Kim and Roush, 1980, Chapter 6). All of these models express the values of the variable in which change is being described as functions of time. *Descriptions* of change in a variable should include only that variable and time in the mathematical formula; *explanations* of change involve the introduction of other variables into the equation.

An example of a deterministic model of change is the *internal-influence diffusion model* (Mahajan and Peterson, 1985). Simple models of the diffusion of an innovation such as the internal-influence diffusion model typically express the cumulative number of adopters of an innovation at a given time as a function of time, expressible in the form a differential equation (Hamblin et al., 1973; Mahajan and Peterson, 1985). One possible equation for describing this process is

$$\frac{dX}{dt} = ct^n$$

where X is the cumulative number who have adopted an innovation, dX/dt is the rate of change in X, t is time measured in some appropriate unit, and n and c are constant parameters that need to be estimated. If we integrate the equation, it may be written equivalently as

$$X = \frac{ct^{n+1}}{n+1}$$

In its simplest form, if $n = 0$, the equation becomes $X = ct$; X is expressed as a linear function of time, and the constant c may be estimated by using ordinary least-squares regression techniques. This approach, or variations with polynomial functions of t, may be useful for describing change when the number of cases is relatively large (e.g., more than 20) and the number of measurement periods is relatively small. This contrasts with time-series analysis (Box and Jenkins, 1970; McCleary and Hay, 1980), in which the number of cases is usually small (typically one case) and the number of measurement periods is typically large (preferably greater than 50).

Time-series analysis is a probabilistic method for describing change in quantitative variables that has become increasingly popular in the social sciences, especially since the publication of Box and Jenkins (1970). Time-series analysis attempts to describe long series of time-ordered data in terms of some combination of four processes. A white noise process is a series of random shocks or changes; this is the probabilistic component that is present in all stochastic time-series models. An autoregressive (AR) process is one in which the present values of a variable depend on past values of that same variable at some specified lag(s) or interval(s). A moving average (MA) process is one in which past values of the white noise process continue to influence present values of the modeled variable for some finite, specified lag(s) or interval(s). An integrated (I) process is one in which there is a detectable trend or drift over time in the values of the modeled variable, but in which there is no trend or drift in the series that results from subtracting values of the variable from values of the variable at some later time. The purpose of subtracting or *differencing* is to obtain a *stationary* white noise time series, one in which the value of the white noise process has a mean of zero (that is, the value of the random component of the series at one time is uncorrelated with the value of that series at another time for any specified time interval). A time-series analysis may incorporate one, two, or all three of the processes in addition to the white noise process in order to obtain a stationary time series, and to describe how a variable changes over time. Time-series analysis has long been used in economic analysis and forecasting, and Vigderhous (1977) has applied time-series analysis to the study of suicide.

Univariate Models of Qualitative Change. Univariate models of change for qualitative data use stage-state analyses or dynamic typologies, classifications into finite sets of categories such that a case may move from one category to another over time. Stage-state models of univariate change are concerned with the probability of moving from one value (state) to another value of a variable by a given period (stage). For multiple category or *multivalent* categorical variables, separate probabilities of *transition* (movement from one value to another in a given interval between periods) are calculated for each pair of *origin* (the state or value at the beginning of the interval) and *destination* (the state or value at the end of the interval) states, including those instances when the origin state is the same as the destination state. When the origin and the destination are the same, the transition probability indicates the stability of membership in that state over the specified interval.

Univariate stage-state models of change in the social sciences are characteristically probabilistic, not deterministic. Stage-state transitions may be described using simple transition matrices, with no assumptions about underlying properties of the transition matrices (Elliott et al., 1989: 179), Markov models, including Markov chains (Bartholomew, 1973; Markus, 1979), log-linear models (Hout, 1983), univariate life table models (Namboodiri and Suchindran, 1987), or univariate survival or hazard models (Allison, 1984; Blossfeld et al., 1989). Life table models and survival or hazard models are generally based on measurements taken for several periods (usually more than 10, occasionally as few as 5). The other models may be based on as few as two periods.

Elliott et al. (1989) used transition matrices to model transitions from nondelinquency to increasing levels of delinquency and drug use in adolescence. They used five stages (1976-1980) and four states (nonoffenders, exploratory offenders, patterned nonserious offenders, and serious offenders for delinquency; nonusers, alcohol users, marijuana users, and polydrug users for drug use). Transition matrices for delinquency were *homogeneous;* they varied from one period to another no more than would be expected based on random error, based on a chi-square test described in Markus (1979). The delinquency matrices for adolescence approximated a stationary Markov process. For drug use, the transition matrices were statistically significantly different from one period to the next, or *nonhomogeneous,* primarily because patterns of transition to higher levels of drug use become more likely in later adolescence than they are in earlier adolescence. Elliott et al. used these transition matrices as part of a larger analysis to describe developmental patterns in illegal behavior. They also used transition matrices to examine the onset or initiation and the suspension of different types of illegal behavior.

Transition matrices, including those involving Markov models and log-linear models, are based on simple row percentages from cross-tabulations or contingency tables that compare the values of a variable at one time (the column variable) for the same set of cases. In the Elliott et al. (1989) example, it was possible to move into or out of each state. In some models, there exist *absorbing states* that, once entered, cannot be left. The most common example of an absorbing state is death. For homogeneous Markov processes with at least one absorbing state, every case will eventually enter an absorbing state, and it is possible to calculate (a) what proportion of cases will be in the absorbing state(s), and each other state, at a given period, and (b) how long it will take all cases, or a certain proportion of cases, to enter the absorbing state(s). Life table models can be used to perform similar calculations. Univariate hazard and survival models are similar to life table models, but assume that the hazard or survival rate follows some fixed distribution. Except for proportional hazards models, that distribution is assumed to be known, and the model may be tested to see how well the data fit the assumed distribution. Survival models have been used to model recidivism (Schmidt and Witte, 1988), labor force participation (Blossfeld et al., 1989), marital history events (Peters, 1988), and other events that involve transitions among discrete states.

Temporal and Causal Order

Earlier, I listed the fundamental requirements for establishing the existence of a causal relationship: covariation, temporal precedence, and nonspuriousness. Two approaches to the issue of causal and temporal order are considered here: stage-state analysis and temporal order of measurement.

When variables can be coded to indicate whether a presumed causal variable or a presumed dependent (effect) variable has changed, stage-state analysis may be used to indicate the temporal order of those changes. These changes may be measured as simple dichotomies (yes, change has occurred, or no, change has not occurred). One important type of change is the *onset* or *initiation* of a particular state or type of behavior. This refers to the first time that a case enters a particular state or, correspondingly, the first time that an individual engages in a particular type of behavior. Other possible changes include *escalation* of behavior (entry of a higher state on an ordinal scale), de-escalation or reduction (entry of a lower state on an ordinal scale), and the *suspension* of behavior (permanent or temporary exit from all states that indicate involvement in a particular kind of behavior).

Research on the National Youth Survey (Elliott et al., 1989; Huizinga et al., 1989; Menard and Elliott, 1990a) has used stage-state analysis to examine the onset, escalation, and suspension of illegal behavior; the onset of drug use and other forms of illegal behavior; and the onset of illegal behavior and of causal variables (involvement with delinquent friends, weakening of beliefs unfavorable to illegal behavior) thought to cause illegal behavior. These stage-state models provided evidence on some long-standing controversies in criminology. An example is the relationship between drug use and other forms of illegal behavior. Three hypotheses suggested by criminologists have been that (a) drug use leads to other types of illegal behavior, (b) other types of illegal behavior lead to drug use, and (c) both drug use and crime are effects of the same set of causes (e.g., weak beliefs in conventional morality, involvement with delinquent or criminal friends). Huizinga et al. (1989) coded each behavior so that in each period each respondent was classified as either *never* having initiated that behavior or as *ever* (even if not currently active) having initiated that behavior. Ever having initiated one behavior, coupled at some time with never having initiated the other, was counted as a case in which the one behavior was temporally prior to the other. Huizinga et al. found that the onset of drug use (including alcohol use) typically followed the onset of other types of illegal behavior (evidence against the hypothesis that drug use, at least initially, leads to other types of crime), but also found that heavy drug use appears to inhibit suspension of serious illegal behavior. It thus appears that drug use is not implicated as a cause of the onset of illegal behavior, but it may be a cause of continuation of illegal behavior.

Stage-state analysis may not always be a feasible approach to the examination of temporal or causal order. In some instances, the process or relationship being investigated has been ongoing for a long time, and it is not possible to collect data on onset. This is a problem of *left-hand censoring,* the failure to detect when a change has occurred because it happened before the first period for which data were collected. Alternatively, the variables being analyzed may have no meaningful onset or suspension. In cross-national models, for example, no nation ever has "zero" economic production or "zero" mortality or fertility at any period in its existence. These are characteristics of a nation that persist through time, and one cannot establish causal or temporal order by asking which started first. Changes in both variables take place from one period to the next, and stage-state models cannot disentangle which is cause and which is effect.

As explained earlier (see Figure 3.1), simply measuring one variable for an earlier period and the other variable for a later period does not establish the first as a cause of the second. Linear panel analysis (Kessler and Greenberg, 1981; Markus, 1979) may be used to help disentangle causal order in studies that involve variables for which there is no meaningful onset, and that are not amenable to stage-state analysis. For example, Menard (1990) used a two-wave panel model to examine the relationship among fertility, mortality, and several indicators of social and economic development. Consistent with demographic transition theory, Menard found that mortality had a substantial positive influence on fertility. Consistent with Malthusian and classical economic theory, a positive effect of economic prosperity (as measured at the national level by per capita gross national product) was also found, but this effect was small. Inconsistent with both Marxian and Malthusian theories, fertility appeared to have no effect, direct or indirect, on economic prosperity or mortality. The use of linear panel analysis with lagged endogenous variables helped separate which variables had effects on which others in the face of theoretical disagreements about causal ordering.

Two important qualifications must be noted about the use of linear panel models for disentangling causal order. First, the lag time (the interval between periods) must be adequate to allow change in one variable to be clearly separated from change in another. This qualification applies to stage-state models as well. If the change in both variables occurs in the same measurement period, it is possible that (a) the two variables are really measuring the same thing; (b) the two variables are spuriously related, and their common causes produce changes in both variables at the same time; and most likely of all (c) the measurement period is too long, and reducing the length of the measurement period would allow us to temporally separate the two changes. Second, in linear panel models, the lag between measurement periods must correspond to the time it takes for the cause to produce an effect. This second criterion for causal lag times is not critical if variables have very stable values over time, but for variables that fluctuate considerably from one period to another, misspecification of the temporal lag between cause and effect may lead to incorrect inferences about the causal order of the cross-sectional variables or, even more likely, about the strength of the relationship between the two. For example, if the specified lag is too short, a strong relationship may appear to be weak because the full effect of changes in the causal variable have not yet been reflected in the dependent variable.

Another issue in the use of stage-state or linear panel models is the use of point and interval measures, A *point* measure is one that is obtained for a single point in time (for example, the day on which the interview occurs). Attitudinal measures are typically point measures. An *interval* measure involves a count of events, or a frequency, measured for an extended interval of time (for example, the year preceding the interview). Many measures of behavior, especially of frequency (how many times) and time span (for how long a period), are interval measures. (This should not be confused with interval *scales,* which are scales with certain measurement properties; interval *measures* are defined in terms of the amount of time over which the measurement is taken.) The fact that a point measure is asked only for a very short span of time (right now) and an interval measure is asked for a very long span of time (all of last year) does not mean that the point measure is valid for the entire year for which it is measured. It is entirely possible, for example, that moral beliefs measured on the day of the interview have been stable for the past 10 months (before which time they changed from stronger to weaker) and that marijuana use reported for the previous year all occurred within the past 8 months (prior to which there was no marijuana use by the respondent). Even though the times for which the measurements were taken might indicate that marijuana use changed before beliefs, the true temporal (and causal, if other conditions are met) order in this example would be that the change in belief preceded the change in marijuana use.

If both stage-state and linear panel analyses are possible, the results may be complementary and may help uncover complex, interactive, or reciprocal relationships that would be undiscovered without a thorough analysis of temporal order. When there are strong theoretical reasons for believing that a certain causal relationship exists, one test of the theory is to verify the existence of the hypothesized temporal order. When competing theories posit different and conflicting causal orderings, analysis of temporal order may provide a strong test (Platt, 1964) of competing theories.

Granger Causality. Another approach that tests for both causal direction and strength of causal influence was proposed by Granger (1969). For two variables X_t and Y_t, both of which can be expressed as stationary time series with zero means,

$$X_t = \sum_{j=1}^{m} a_j X_{t-j} + \sum_{j=1}^{m} b_j Y_{t-j} + e_t$$

and

$$Y_t = \sum_{j=1}^{m} c_j X_{t-j} + \sum_{j=1}^{m} d_j Y_{t-j} + f_t$$

where e_t and f_t are taken to be two uncorrelated white noise series, and m is greater than zero but less than the length of the time series.

According to the criterion of Granger causality, Y causes X if some b_j does not equal zero (implicitly, b_j must be statistically significantly different from zero). Correspondingly, X causes Y if some c_j is not equal to zero. In effect, the question posed by the test for Granger causality becomes, "Is there variation in one variable that cannot be explained by past values of that variable, but can be explained by past values of another variable?" If the answer is yes, then the second variable "Granger-causes" the first.

Notice that if $m = 1$, and if there are only two periods in the series, the test for Granger causality reduces to a test for the statistical significance of the coefficients of exogenous variables (all measured at time 1) on the endogenous variable (measured at time 2) when the lagged endogenous variable (measured at time 1) is included in the equation. In other words, Y_2 is modeled as a function of Y_1 and X_1 (and there may be more than one X variable measured at time 1). Instantaneous effects (e.g., from X_2 to Y_2) are excluded from the model. This amounts to a two-wave panel model with no instantaneous effects, like that used by Menard (1990) in the analysis of fertility, mortality, family planning, and development.

The choice of m is arbitrary within the limits imposed by the length of the time series. Barnard and Krautmann (1988) used a single lagged endogenous variable (Y_{t-1}) with X measured at three periods (X_{t-1}, X_{t-2}, and X_{t-3}). Sims (1972) used lags of length 8, and also used "future lags" (in effect allowing future values of Y to influence the current value of Y). To be a cause of Y in Sims's model, X must explain variation in Y that is unexplained by both past and future values of Y. Wright (1989) separately analyzed lags of 1, 2, 3, 4, and 5 for the endogenous variable. There is some inconsistency in the results for different lags when this approach is taken. For example, Granger causality may be confirmed at lags of 3 and 4, but not at lags of 1, 2, or 5. How are we to interpret such results?

In general, the more prior values of the endogenous variable are in the equation, the greater is the likelihood of rejecting the hypothesis of Granger causality, but the inclusion of additional values of the endogenous variable may have no significant effect beyond some number. This number may be estimated by modeling the endogenous variable as an autoregressive time series, or by calculating separate ordinary least-squares regression models and examining the change in the explained variance (R^2) produced by the inclusion of each additional lagged endogenous variable (e.g., by the addition of Y_{t-4}). If there is no statistically significant change in the explained variance (see, e.g., the test suggested in Agresti and Finlay, 1986: 372-375), there would seem to be little point in including this term in the equation. It may well be that a lag of 1 is sufficient both to explain the variance in the dependent variable and to reject the hypothesis of Granger causality. If so, there may be little point in proceeding beyond lag 1.

It is possible that X_t and Y_t will not be stationary time series. Without sufficient measurements for ARIMA time-series analysis, it may not be possible to determine whether the conditions for applying the Granger test have been met. There seem to be ample possibilities for misusing the test, and the assumption of stationarity should not be taken for granted. Caution should be taken, particularly when applying the test to data for which the usual ARIMA time-series methods are not applicable.

Cross-Sectional Data and Causal Order. Methods have been developed to attempt to resolve the issue of causal order when only cross-sectional data are available. Simon (1954), Lazarsfeld (1955), and Blalock (1962) have proposed the use of partial correlation techniques to test assumptions about causal order. These methods can, in principle, be extended to include hypotheses about multiple regression coefficients (Van de Geer, 1971) in cross-sectional data. They depend on the elimination, *a priori*, based on theory, of causal relationships in certain directions between certain variables. They are incapable of resolving the issue of temporal order, and they may be confounded by even moderately complex relationships. For example, given two variables, X and Y, each of which is thought to influence the other, the cross-sectional partial correlation methods cannot test whether Y causes X, X causes Y, or both (each causes the other). By contrast, stage-state analysis, linear panel analysis, and Granger causality analysis are all capable of providing evidence about the true causal order between X and Y, given appropriate longitudinal data.

Two-stage least-squares (2SLS) methods (Berry, 1984; Heise, 1975; Kessler and Greenberg, 1981; Markus, 1979) may be used with cross-sectional data to model *nonrecursive* causal relationships, relationships that involve reciprocal influence or "feedback" within some set of two or more variables. In cross-sectional 2SLS models, problems of model identification may arise if *instrumental variables* cannot be uniquely estimated. In panel designs, the problem may be solved by using *future* values of predictors to estimate an instrumental variable for the *current* value of a variable. Counterintuitive though this may seem, it is appropriate in a situation when the only purpose is to construct an unbiased estimate of a variable, X_t, that is uncorrelated with measurement error in X at time t. This variable may then be used to estimate the effects of X_t on other variables, but there will be some loss of precision in these estimates (Kessler and Greenberg, 1981). Unless there are problems of autocorrelated error in panel data, 2SLS estimation may be neither necessary nor desirable. To return to the main point, however, longitudinal data provide more flexible and more generally applicable methods for examining causal order than those possible with cross-sectional data.

Longitudinal methods of examining temporal and causal order are most appropriate for use with total population or panel data. They may be useful for repeated cross-sectional data at the group or aggregate level, with the same qualifications noted in the section on Other Issues in the Measurement of Change regarding the measurement of change in repeated cross-sectional designs. Ideally, stage-state methods would be used to ascertain temporal order, and Granger tests or linear panel analysis would also be used to test the magnitude and direction of causal influences.

Causal Analysis

Causal analysis[5] of longitudinal data involves the extension of change models to encompass independent variables in addition to or instead of time, and sometimes the incorporation of time into techniques for analyzing cross-sectional models, either by incorporating some measure of time as a variable, or by making use of two or more waves of data to ensure that a supposed cause is measured at an appropriate interval prior to its supposed effect. There are four "pure" types of longitudinal models: (a) the value of the dependent variable(s) is expressed as a function of the value(s) of the independent variables; (b) the value of the dependent variable(s) is expressed as a function of the change in the independent variable(s); (c) the change in the dependent variables is expressed as a function of the value of the independent variable(s); and (d) the change in the dependent variable(s) is expressed as a function of the change in the independent variable(s). Mixed models, in which (for example) the independent variables include both level and rate-of-change variables (e.g., population density and population growth rate as influences on economic development) are also possible.

In causal analysis with cross-sectional data, we often phrase our hypotheses as though we were testing model D: a change in X produces (leads to, causes) a change in Y. More typically, however, it is model A that we test in cross-sectional *and* longitudinal analysis. Correctly phrased, model A indicates that the *level* or value of one variable (the dependent variable) depends on the level or value of one or more independent variables. This *implies* that a change in the dependent variable is also a function of change(s) in the independent variable(s), but the actual formulation of the model to be tested involves values of variables, not changes in values. In addition, it is possible that a change in one variable produces a systematic change in another, but that the values of the two variables are largely unrelated. This suggests a process in which the initial values of X and Y were independent, but changes in X produce changes in Y. For example, levels of nutrition (as measured by per capita calorie supply) may initially be unrelated to levels of national family planning program effort (countries with both high and low levels of nutrition have both high and low levels of family planning program effort), but increases in family planning program effort may lead to increases in per capita calorie supply, as individuals more effectively adjust their fertility, deliberately or inadvertently, to the carrying capacity of their country or region. High levels of family planning program effort are still not necessarily associated with high levels of nutrition, but improvements in family planning program effort are associated with improvements in nutrition. The process described here is admittedly counterintuitive, but nonetheless possible. If such a process exists, then model D is appropriate, but model A is not.

Model D, on the other hand, may be appropriate in any situation for which A is appropriate. If the level of one variable depends on the level of another, then if the second variable changes, the first must also (i.e., the change in the first variable depends on the change in the second, if model A is correct). Analytically, model D may result from the use of first difference models, as suggested by Liker et al. (1985). In a first difference model, all variables in the model are expressed as raw gain scores.

An example of the pure form of model B might be the correspondence between the level of stress (as a dependent variable) and the amount of change in income (a big pay raise reduces stress, a big pay cut increases stress, regardless of level of income). Model C is the standard form for differential equation models. For example, Richardson (1960) explained arms races between pairs of countries by using pairs of differential equations:

$$\frac{dX}{dt} = kY - aX + g \quad \text{and} \quad \frac{dY}{dt} = jX - bY + h$$

where X and Y represent levels of armaments in the two countries, j and k represent nonnegative "defense" coefficients (positive influences on the felt need for arms, based on the level of armaments in the other country), a and b represented nonnegative "fatigue" coefficients (the drain on the national economy, or unwillingness to build up one's own armaments further, given the level of armaments already present in one's own country), and g and h are constant, positive or negative "grievance" factors that may loosely be interpreted as the hostility (if they are positive) or friendliness (if they are negative) each country feels toward the other. The right-hand side of the equations, dX/dt and dY/dt, are rates of change over time; the left-hand side of the equations are expressed in terms of levels of the variables X and Y.

Model C was also used by Mauldin and Berelson (1978) in a regression analysis to explain changes in crude birthrates in less developed countries. With change in crude birthrate as the dependent variable, levels of family planning program effort and indicators of social and economic development were used as the independent variables. Tsui and Bogue (1978) performed a similar analysis with similar variables, but used model A with a lagged endogenous variable. As Markus (1979) explains, the use of a gain score as the dependent variable is the same as using a lagged endogenous variable except that in the model with the gain score as the dependent variable, the coefficient of the lagged endogenous variable is assumed to be one. For the lagged endogenous model with dependent variable Y and independent variable X,

$$Y_2 = a + bX + cY_1$$

recalculating,

$$Y_2 - cY_1 = a + bX$$

If $c = 1$, then the equation takes the form of a standard regression model, with the gain score $(Y_2 - Y_1)$ as the dependent variable. Given the similarity in the gain score and lagged endogenous approaches, it is not surprising that Mauldin and Berelson (1978) and Tsui and Bogue (1978) reached practically identical substantive conclusions; even the explained variance in the dependent variables was practically identical. Markus (1979) suggests that there is nothing to be gained by constraining the coefficient c in the above model to be equal to one, and recommends the use of the lagged endogenous variable instead of the gain score as a dependent variable. This recommendation is consistent with the recommendations of Cronbach and Furby (1970), but as already noted, Liker et al. (1985) offer a dissenting view.

Methods of Causal Analysis of Longitudinal Data. All of the methods used for cross-sectional data analysis may be used with equal facility (and with equal concern for the underlying assumptions and limitations of those methods) in the analysis of longitudinal data. Simple frequencies; measures of association, dispersion, and central tendency; and contingency table methods are all applicable to longitudinal data. So, too, are parametric and nonparametric tests for statistical significance. Multivariate (or multivariable; see Kleinbaum et al., 1988) methods may also be used. The principal difference is that in longitudinal analysis the methods may be used on time-ordered data, and may be used to analyze variation in a single variable measured for two or more periods, instead of two or more variables measured for a single period.

Table 5.1 presents some appropriate methods of analysis for different combinations, in terms of level of measurement, of dependent and independent variables. Latent variable structural equation models (Bollen, 1989; Hayduk, 1987) have become a standard in both cross-sectional and longitudinal data analysis. Linear panel analysis (Kessler and Greenberg, 1981) and multiple regression and path analysis (Heise, 1975; Johnston, 1984; Kleinbaum et al., 1988) may be regarded as special cases of the broader latent variable structural equation model. When both dependent and independent variables are measured on a continuous scale, and when the number of periods for which the variables are measured is large, transfer function or multivariate time series (Box and Jenkins, 1970; McCleary and Hay, 1980) may be appropriate. Alternatively, spectral analysis, a variant of time-series analysis (Jenkins and Watts, 1968; Wei, 1990) may be appropriate for problems involving predictions to one time series from one or more other time series.

With categorical or mixed variables as predictors of a continuous dependent variable, analysis of variance (ANOVA) for categorical predictors with analysis of covariance (ANCOVA) for continuous predictors may be appropriate if the data satisfy the assumptions of homogeneity of variance and equal cell sizes (Bohrnstedt and Knoke, 1982; Iversen and Norpoth, 1987; Wildt and Ahtola, 1978). Dummy variable regression is a variant of ANOVA that may also be worth considering. If there is one categorical predictor and a dependent variable that is at least ordinal, nonparametric methods analogous to ANOVA may be worth considering; for example, Friedman two-way analysis of variance or Kruskal-Wallis one-way analysis of variance (Daniel, 1978; Siegel, 1956).

In regression analysis and related methods, longitudinal analysis may give rise to problems that are somewhat different from those encountered in cross-sectional regression analysis. Autocorrelated error is a potential problem in both cross-sectional and longitudinal models; in cross-sectional models, it may be tested using the Durbin-Watson statistic, but for lagged

TABLE 5.1
Methods of Analysis for Longitudinal Data

Dependent variable	Independent variable	Methods of analysis
Quantitative/ continuous	Quantitative/ continuous	Differential equations; Regression; Multivariate ARIMA time-series analysis; Latent variable structural equation models
	Mixed continuous and categorical	ANOVA with ANCOVA; Regression with dummy variables
	Qualitative/ categorical	ANOVA; Nonparametric ANOVA; Dummy variable regression
Qualitative/categorical	Quantitative/continuous	Discriminant analysis; Logit or probit analysis; Logistic regression; Hazard/survival/ event history analysis
	Mixed continuous and categorical	Log-linear analysis; Logistic regression; Hazard/survival/ event history analysis
	Qualitative/ categorical	Log-linear analysis; Multistate life table models; Hazard/ survival/event history analysis

endogenous variables, a modification of the Durbin-Watson test is required (Johnston, 1984). In latent variable structural equation models, correlated error may be modeled within the analysis, but unless the model is correctly specified, it may fail to converge, or may produce nonsensical parameter estimates (e.g., negative variance estimates). Collinearity is also as much or more a problem in longitudinal analysis as in cross-sectional analysis. Potentially, problems of model specification are magnified, not reduced, in longitudinal analysis.

For categorical dependent variables, the same techniques that are used for cross-sectional analysis may also be used for longitudinal analysis: discriminant analysis (Klecka, 1980; Kleinbaum et al., 1988; Van de Geer, 1971) or logit models (Aldrich and Nelson, 1984) for continuous independent variables, and log-linear models (Knoke and Burke, 1980; Lindeman et al., 1980) for categorical or mixed independent variables. If the dependent variable is a measure of *change* in a categorical variable, then multistate life table models (Namboodiri and Suchindran, 1987) for categorical predictors, and event history analysis (Allison, 1984; Blossfeld et al., 1989; Cox and Oakes, 1984; Namboodiri and Suchindran, 1987) for continuous, categorical, or mixed independent variables, provide powerful tools for the analysis of stage-state change. Event history analysis is a family of methods that links regression analysis and the analysis of transition matrices for data that include measurements at several periods. Event history analysis typically allows more predictors and requires fewer periods than ARIMA time-series analysis can conveniently or meaningfully handle. It also allows the use of either age or chronological time as the underlying time continuum, and the use of the other time variable as an independent variable, so that both historical and developmental trends may be examined. Multistate life table models may, in a sense, be regarded as a nonparametric form of event history analysis. They analyze stage-state transitions without making any assumptions about the underlying temporal distribution of those transitions (as in event history analysis), and in that sense are more flexible than event history analysis, but they also have greater difficulty handling large numbers of independent variables. All of these analytical methods are applicable to total population and panel data, and, with caution, to aggregated categories or groups of cases in repeated cross-sectional data.

Longitudinal and Cross-Sectional Data Analysis. Assume that we have selected a theoretically appropriate set of dependent and independent variables. Assume further that we have agreed upon the causal ordering of the variables, based on theory and perhaps with empirical support based on past research. Assume further that we have been able, with appropriate transformations of our variables, to cast the causal model into a general linear model (e.g., latent variable structural equations, multiple regression, ANOVA and ANCOVA, or discriminant analysis), and that the model is identified (see Heise, 1975, for a discussion of model identification). Suppose now that we want to calculate the strength of the direct causal relationships (and if we use path analysis or latent variable structural equation models, we may also calculate indirect effects). Is there any reason to prefer longitudinal data instead of cross-sectional data for this purpose?

Schoenberg (1977) demonstrated that under certain conditions, the application of dynamic models to cross-sectional data produced efficient, unbiased estimates of the parameters of the underlying dynamic model. The fundamental condition for this to occur was that the underlying dynamic process be *nonergodic,* that is, that it depend on the initial state of the system. For *ergodic* systems, systems that do not depend on the initial state of the system, but that would result in an identical expected state of the system for any time period, the calculation of a dynamic model based on cross-sectional data results in biased and inefficient estimates of parameters.

An example of an ergodic system is one in which changes in the exogenous variables are random, and the expected values of the exogenous variables are the same at any time t as at any other time $(t - k)$. Mathematically, $E(X_t) = X_0$, where X_0 is the initial value of X. An example of a nonergodic system is one in which changes in the independent variables are not random but depend on past values of the exogenous variable. In other words, an autoregressive process, in addition to random variation, generates the values of the exogenous variables, and the expected value of X is not constant. Mathematically, $E(X_t) = FX_{t-k}$, where X_{t-k} is a vector of past values of X and F is a vector of coefficients for X. Whether cross-sectional data may be used to calculate the dynamic relationship between the exogenous variables (X) and the dependent variable (Y) would depend on which process, random variation or autoregression, produced the changes in X. By contrast, longitudinal models may be used for both ergodic and nonergodic processes.

A second potential problem with using cross-sectional data to estimate parameters for a longitudinal model is illustrated by Firebaugh (1980) with data on fertility and literacy. Table 5.2 and Figure 5.1, both adapted from Firebaugh (1980: 340-341), illustrate that cross-sectional and longitudinal correlations may be opposite in sign, and yet may both be correct. Cross-sectionally, fertility was highest in those districts of the Punjab in India with the highest levels of literacy, beginning in 1961 and continuing through 1971. Within each district, however, as literacy increased over time, fertility declined. In this example, cross-sectional and longitudinal data produce very different conclusions about the relationship between fertility and literacy. This same point was illustrated by Menard and Elliott (1990a) and Greenberg (1985) with regard to the relationship between age and illegal behavior. As Firebaugh remarks, determining which of the two patterns is more appropriate or important is a theoretical issue, not an empirical issue, but the point here is that cross-sectional data cannot be routinely used to model dynamic, longitudinal relationships. This point is further reinforced by Menard and Elliott (1990a) based on actual cross-sectional and longitudinal data, and by Davies and Pickles (1985), who demonstrated in a simulation study of a

TABLE 5.2

Cross-Sectional and Longitudinal Correlations Between Fertility
and Literacy: the Punjab, India, 1961-1971

Time-series correlations (within districts over time)		Cross-sectional correlations (within years across districts)	
District	Correlation	Year	Correlation
Amritsar	−.9	1961	.5
Bhatinda	−.5	1962	.6
Ferozepur	−.9	1963	.4
Gurdaspur	−.9	1964	.6
Hoshiarpur	−.8	1965	.1
Jullundur	−.7	1966	.2
Kapurthala	−.4	1967	.3
Ludhiana	−.9	1968	.6
Patiala	−.3	1969	.5
Ropar	−.4	1970	.6
Sangrur	−.1	1971	.7

dynamic model that cross-sectional analysis failed to make correct inferences about predefined population parameters, but longitudinal analysis estimates were well within the limits of sampling error.

Longitudinal Versus Cross-Sectional Data and Analysis

This monograph began by contrasting pure cross-sectional research with longitudinal research, and did so for the purpose of defining longitudinal research. It ends now by summarizing the differences between the two.

(1) Longitudinal research typically costs more. If the research question or hypothesis can be addressed satisfactorily with cross-sectional data, there is little or no point in trying to use longitudinal research to answer the research question or test the hypothesis.

(2) Longitudinal research has the same problems and issues of data quality and adequacy of sampling as cross-sectional research, and a few more besides. There are ways of addressing these issues, but again if cross-sectional research is adequate to the task, it is to be preferred over longitudinal research.

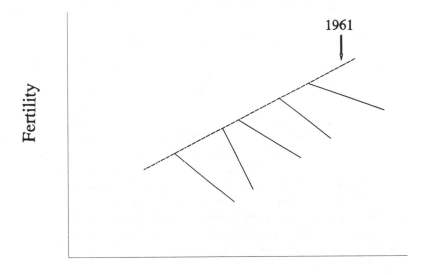

Figure 5.1 General Pattern of the Relationship between Fertility and Literacy

(3) Cross-sectional research cannot disentangle developmental (age) trends, historical (period) trends, and cohort effects. Whenever all three types of effects are possible, the study of any or all of these three types of change requires longitudinal data.

(4) The description and analysis of historical change absolutely requires the use of longitudinal data; also, longitudinal methods of analysis such as differential equation models (in which differentiation is performed with respect to time), ARIMA time-series models, and event history analysis may provide more powerful and detailed analyses of historical change than would those methods common to both longitudinal and cross-sectional analysis.

(5) The description and analysis of developmental trends may be attempted with cross-sectional age-specific (or stage-specific) data, but the results will not necessarily reflect those obtained by using longitudinal data. Insofar as

developmental change is conceived as reflecting the experience of individuals as they age or pass through successive stages, longitudinal data, because they reflect intraindividual change rather than interindividual differences, are to be preferred.

(6) Unless there is good reason to believe otherwise (e.g., unless it is known that a dynamic process is nonergodic), it should be assumed that longitudinal data are necessary to estimate the parameters, efficiently and without bias, of any dynamic process in the social sciences.

(7) Unless recall periods are short, or problems of respondent conditioning are severe, or unless it can be demonstrated that problems of long-term recall are minor or nonexistent, prospective panel designs or total population designs are generally to be preferred over other longitudinal designs.

(8) Testing for temporal or causal order should be an integral component in testing causal hypotheses. Along with covariation (as indicated by the strength of the relationship) and nonspuriousness (as indicated by the continued significance of the relationship when the effects of other variables are considered), temporal or causal order, as indicated in stage-state temporal order analysis, Granger causality, or linear panel analysis, is a crucial element in any causal relationship.

In light of these conclusions, what role remains to cross-sectional research? The most readily apparent answer is that cross-sectional research remains important for describing variables and patterns of relationships as they exist at a particular time. Cross-sectional research must also be considered as a relatively less expensive alternative to longitudinal research for those instances in which cross-sectional research is a demonstrably adequate substitute for longitudinal research, and for exploratory or preliminary investigation of hypotheses or research questions that involve dynamic models. If the concern is with differences between individuals of different ages at one time, and not with inferring intraindividual changes that occur with age over the life course, cross-sectional research is again preferable. The conclusion is inescapable, however, that for the description and analysis of dynamic change processes, longitudinal research is ultimately indispensable. It is also the case that longitudinal research can, in principle, do much that cross-sectional research cannot, but that there is little or nothing that cross-sectional research can, in principle, do that longitudinal research cannot.

Longitudinal research is not the cure for all the problems of cross-sectional research. It cannot cure problems of poor research design (quite the contrary — it is likely to magnify such problems), inadequate sampling, or failure to pay attention to the assumptions and limitations of analytical techniques. Longitudinal research is not an absolute necessity for all research problems;

there is much that has been done and much that can be accomplished with cross-sectional research. Longitudinal research is best viewed as a powerful tool, but only one of several that is available to the social scientist. If the research question or hypothesis does require longitudinal data and analysis, then the costs of longitudinal research, if longitudinal research is used well, are likely to be amply compensated by the quality of the results.

NOTES

1. For a discussion of the use of social indicators and a presentation of some indicators of social change, see Bauer (1966), Sheldon and Moore (1968), and Taeuber (1981).

2. One might suggest additional criteria as well. For instance, one might insist on some mechanism or linkage that connects cause with effect. This is a rather vague criterion, and in the social sciences may suggest no more than a set of intervening variables. In the physical sciences, it may consist of a rejection in principle of "action at a distance," i.e., in order for one mass/energy cluster to affect another mass/energy cluster, there must be some contact, some exchange of a particle or wave; but quantum theory apparently implies the existence of action at a distance. Thomsen (1987) writes that "quantum mechanical causality is statistical, and it applies to large ensembles of individuals. Its probabilities are usually between 0 and 1, and the customary interpretation of them is that a certain fraction of the individuals will do one thing and a certain fraction something else." This description of causality, along with the assertion that "quantum mechanics cannot make predictions about individual objects," is consistent with the idea of causality as it is used in the social sciences, and the allowance of action at a distance would seem to eliminate the need for a fourth criterion of causality (mechanism or linkage). For a more extended treatment of the topic of causality, see Blalock (1964, 1971), Heise (1975), Nagel (1961), and Williamson et al. (1982). For a dissenting view that suggests that the term *causality* is improperly used and unnecessary for investigation in the social sciences, see Kerlinger (1986: 361).

3. If N is the number of cases across all periods and T is the number of periods for which data are available for the cases, then if $N(T - 1)$ cases would be sufficient to allow the use of a particular method (e.g., tests for the statistical significance of differences in means, or multiple regression with three or four independent variables), it may be appropriate to pool the cross-sectional and time-series data into a single two- or three-wave longitudinal analysis. Kessler and Greenberg (1981) and Sayrs (1989) discuss methods for pooling cross-sectional and time-series data, and both agree that other methods are preferable if the numbers of cases and periods are not too small.

4. In particular, high scores that are high (and low scores that are low) because of random error will tend to decrease (increase) to the mean; this is the phenomenon variously called regression to the mean, the regression effect, or statistical regression (Kerlinger, 1986: 296-298; Kessler and Greenberg, 1981: 16-17; Lindeman et al., 1980: 17). More generally, gain scores tend to be negatively correlated with random error: Scores that are high (or low) because they are inflated (or deflated) by random error in one period will tend to be lower (higher) in another period, once the effects of random error (by definition uncorrelated from one period to another) are absent. Positive random error is thus associated with a negative gain score and negative random error is associated with a positive gain score.

5. For basic discussions of causal modeling, see Asher (1976), Davis (1985), Blalock (1964), and Heise (1975). For an approach from the philosophy of science, see Nagel (1961). For a good general discussion of bivariate and multivariate methods of analysis, see Kleinbaum et al. (1988), Lindeman et al. (1980), or Van de Geer (1971). Regarding specific techniques, see also the sources cited in the text.

REFERENCES

AGRESTI, A. AND FINLAY, B. (1986) Statistical Methods for the Social Sciences. San Francisco: Dellen.

AHLUWALIA, M. S. (1974) "Income inequality: Some dimensions of the problem," in H. B. Chenery, M. S. Ahluwalia, C. L. G. Bell, J. H. Duloy, and R. Jolly (eds.) Redistribution with Growth: An Approach to Policy. Oxford, UK: Oxford University Press.

AHLUWALIA, M. S. (1976) "Inequality, poverty, and development." Journal of Development Economics 3: 307-342.

ALDRICH, J. H. and NELSON, F. D. (1984) Linear Probability, Logit and Probit Models. Beverly Hills, CA: Sage.

ALLISON, P. D. (1984) Event History Analysis: Regression for Longitudinal Event Data. Beverly Hills, CA: Sage.

APPLEMAN, P. (ed.). (1976) Thomas Robert Malthus: An Essay on the Principle of Population. New York: Norton.

ASHER, H. B. (1976) Causal Modeling. Beverly Hills, CA: Sage.

BABBIE, E. (1989) The Practice of Social Research (5th ed.). Belmont, CA: Wadsworth.

BAILEY, K. D. (1987) Methods of Social Research (3rd ed.). New York: Macmillan.

BALTES, P. B., CORNELIUS, S. W. and NESSELROADE, J. R. (1979) "Cohort effects in developmental psychology," in J. R. Nesselroade and P. B. Baltes (eds.) Longitudinal Research in the Study of Behavior and Development. New York: Academic Press.

BALTES, P. B. and NESSELROADE, J. R. (1979) "History and rationale of longitudinal research," in J. R. Nesselroade and P. B. Baltes (eds.) Longitudinal Research in the Study of Behavior and Development. New York: Academic Press.

BARNARD, J. R. and KRAUTMANN, A. C. (1988) "Population growth among U.S. regions and metropolitan areas: A test for causality." Journal of Regional Science 28: 103-118.

BARTHOLOMEW, D. J. (1973) Stochastic Models for Social Processes (2nd ed.). New York: John Wiley.

BAUER, R. A. (ed.) (1966) Social Indicators. Cambridge: MIT Press.

BECKER, G. S., LANDES, E. M. and MICHAEL, F. T. (1977) "An economic analysis of marital instability." Journal of Political Economy 85: 1141-1187.

BERRUETA-CLEMENT, J., SCHWEINHART, L. J. BARNETT, W. S. EPSTEIN, A. S. and WEIKART, D. P. (1984) Changed Lives: The Effects of the Perry Preschool Program on Youths Through Age 19. Ypsilanti, MI: High/Scope Educational Research Foundation.

BERRY, W. D. (1984) Nonrecursive Causal Models. Beverly Hills, CA: Sage.

BLACK, C. E. (1966) The Dynamics of Modernization. New York: Harper & Row.

BLALOCK, A. B. and BLALOCK, H. M., Jr. (1982) An Introduction to Social Research. Englewood Cliffs, NJ: Prentice-Hall.

BLALOCK, H. M., Jr. (1962) "Four-variable causal models and partial correlations." American Journal of Sociology 68: 182-194.

BLALOCK, H. M., Jr. (1964) Causal Inference in Nonexperimental Research. New York: Norton.

74

BLALOCK, H. M., Jr. (1969) Theory Construction: From Verbal to Mathematical Formulations. Englewood Cliffs, NJ: Prentice-Hall.

BLALOCK, H. M., Jr. (1971) Causal Models in the Social Sciences. Chicago: Aldine.

BLAU, P. M. and DUNCAN, O. D. (1966) The American Occupational Structure. New York: John Wiley.

BLOSSFELD, H., HAMERLE, A. and MAYER, K. U. (1989) Event History Analysis: Statistical Theory and Application in the Social Sciences. Hillsdale, NJ: Lawrence Erlbaum.

BLUMSTEIN, A., COHEN, J., ROTH, J. A., and VISHER, C. A. (eds.) (1986) Criminal Careers and "Career Criminals." Volumes I and II. Washington, DC: National Academy Press.

BOHRNSTEDT, G. W. and KNOKE, D. (1982) Statistics for Social Data Analysis. Itasca, IL: F. E. Peacock.

BOLLEN, K. A. (1989) Structural Equations with Latent Variables. New York: John Wiley.

BOX, G. E. P. and JENKINS, G. M. (1970) Time Series Analysis: Forecasting and Control. San Francisco: Holden-Day.

BULMER, M. G. (1979) Principles of Statistics. New York: Dover.

BURGESS, R. D. (1989) "Major issues and implications of tracing survey respondents," in D. Kasprzyk, G. Duncan, G. Kalton, and M. P. Singh (eds.) Panel Surveys. New York: John Wiley.

CALDWELL, J. C. (1976) "Toward a restatement of demographic transition theory." Population and Development Review 2: 321-366.

CAMPBELL, D. T. and STANLEY, J. C. (1963) Experimental and Quasi-Experimental Designs for Research. Chicago: Rand McNally.

CANTOR, D. (1989) "Substantive implications of longitudinal design features: The National Crime Survey as a case study," in D. Kasprzyk, G. Duncan, G. Kalton, and M. P. Singh (eds.) Panel Surveys. New York: John Wiley.

CARLSON, E. (1979) "Divorce rate fluctuation as a cohort phenomenon." Population Studies 33: 523-536.

CHILTON, R. and SPIELBERGER, A. (1971) "Is delinquency increasing? Age structure and the crime rate." Social Forces 49: 487-493.

CLARRIDGE, B. R., SHEEHY, L. L. and HAUSER, T. (1977) "Tracing members of a panel: A 17-year follow-up," in K. F. Schuessler (ed.) Sociological Methodology 1978. San Francisco: Jossey-Bass.

COLLINS, C., GIVEN, B. and BERRY, D. (1989) "Longitudinal studies as intervention." Nursing Research 38: 251-253.

COVEY, H. C. and MENARD, S. (1987) "Trends in arrests among the elderly." The Gerontologist 27: 666-672.

COVEY, H. C. and MENARD, S. (1988) "Trends in elderly criminal victimization from 1973-1984." Research on Aging 10: 329-341.

COX, D. R. and OAKES, D. (1984) Analysis of Survival Data. London: Chapman and Hall.

CRONBACH, L. J. and FURBY, L. (1970) "How should we measure change — or should we?" Psychological Bulletin 74: 68-80.

DANIEL, W. W. (1978) Applied Nonparametric Statistics. Boston: Houghton Mifflin.

DAVIES, R. B. and PICKLES, A. R. (1985) "Longitudinal versus cross-sectional methods for behavioral research: A first-round knockout." Environment and Planning A 17: 1315-1329.

DAVIS, J. A. (1985) The Logic of Causal Order. Beverly Hills, CA: Sage.

DAVIS, K. (1963) "The theory of change and response in modern demographic history." Population Index 24: 345-366.

EASTERLIN, R. A. (1987) Birth and Fortune (2nd ed.). Chicago: University of Chicago Press.

ELLIOTT, D. S., AGETON, S. S., HUIZINGA, D., KNOWLES, B. A. and CANTER, R. J. (1983) The Prevalence and Incidence of Delinquent Behavior: 1976-1980. Boulder, CO: Behavioral Research Institute.

ELLIOTT, D. S., HUIZINGA, D. and AGETON, S. S. (1985) Explaining Delinquency and Drug Use. Beverly Hills, CA: Sage.

ELLIOTT, D. S., HUIZINGA, D. and MENARD, S. (1989) Multiple Problem Youth: Delinquency, Substance Use, and Mental Health Problems. New York: Springer-Verlag.

FEDERAL BUREAU OF INVESTIGATION (annual) Uniform Crime Reports. Washington, DC: Government Printing Office.

FIREBAUGH, G. (1980) "Cross national versus historical regression models: Conditions of equivalence in comparative analysis." Comparative Social Research 3: 333-344.

FREEMAN, D. (1983) Margaret Mead and Samoa: The Making and Unmaking of an Anthropological Myth. Cambridge, MA: Harvard University Press.

GIST, N. P. and FAVA, S. F. (1974) Urban Society (6th ed.). New York: Crowell/Harper & Row.

GLENN, N. (1976) "Cohort analysts' futile quest: Statistical attempts to separate age, period, and cohort effects." American Sociological Review 41: 900-904.

GLENN, N. (1977) Cohort Analysis. Beverly Hills, CA: Sage.

GOLD, M. and REIMER, D. J. (1975) "Changing patterns of delinquent behavior among Americans 13 through 16 years old: 1967-1972." Crime and Delinquency Literature 7: 483-577.

GRAETZ, B. (1987) "Cohort changes in educational inequality." Social Science Research 16: 329-344.

GRANGER, C. W. J. (1969) "Investigating causal relations by econometric models and cross-spectral methods." Econometrica 37: 424-438.

GREENBERG, D. F. (1985) "Age, crime, and social explanation." American Journal of Sociology 91: 1-21.

HAMBLIN, R.L., JACOBSEN, R. B. and MILLER, J. L. L. (1973) A Mathematical Theory of Social Change. New York: John Wiley.

HARTFORD, R. B. (1984) "The case of the elusive infant mortality rate." Population Today 4: 6-7.

HAYDUK, L. A. (1987) Structural Modeling with LISREL: Essentials and Advances. Baltimore: Johns Hopkins University Press.

HEISE, D. R. (1975) Causal Analysis. New York: John Wiley.

HEYNS, B. (1978) Summer Learning and the Effects of Schooling. New York: Academic Press.

HOBCRAFT, J., MENKEN, J. and PRESTON, S. (1982) "Age, period, and cohort effects in demography: A review." Population Index 48: 4-43.

HOUT, M. (1983) Mobility Tables. Beverly Hills, CA: Sage.

HUCKFELDT, R. R., KOHFELD, C. W. and LIKENS, T. W. (1982) Dynamic Modeling: An Introduction. Beverly Hills, CA: Sage.

HUIZINGA, D.H., MENARD, S. and ELLIOTT, D. S. (1989) "Delinquency and drug use: Temporal and developmental patterns." Justice Quarterly 6: 419-455.

IVERSEN, G. R. and NORPOTH, H. (1987) Analysis of Variance (2nd ed.). Newbury Park, CA: Sage.

JENKINS, G. M. and WATTS, D. G. (1968) Spectral Analysis and its Applications. San Francisco: Holden-Day.

JOHNSTON, J. (1984) Econometric Methods (3rd ed.). New York: McGraw-Hill.

76

JOHNSTON, L. D., BACHMAN, J. G. and O'MALLEY, P. M. (annual) Monitoring the Future: Questionnaire Responses from the Nation's High School Seniors. Ann Arbor, MI: Institute for Social Research.

KALTON, G., KASPRZYK, D. and McMILLEN, D. B. (1989) "Nonsampling errors in panel surveys," in D. G. Kasprzyk, G. Duncan, G. Kalton, and M. P. Singh (eds.) Panel Surveys. New York: John Wiley.

KANDEL, D. B. (1975) "Stages of adolescent involvement in drug use." Science 190: 912-914.

KANDEL, D. B. and FAUST, R. (1975) "Sequence and states in patterns of adolescent drug use." Archives of General Psychiatry 32: 923-932.

KANDEL, D. B. and LOGAN, J. A. (1984) "Patterns of drug use from adolescence to young adulthood I: Periods of risk for initiation, continued use, and discontinuation." American Journal of Public Health 74: 660-666.

KELLING, G. L., PATE, T., DIECKMAN, D. E. and BROWN, C.E. (1974) The Kansas City Preventative Patrol Experiment: A Summary Report. Washington, DC: The Police Foundation

KERLINGER, F. N. (1986) Foundations of Behavioral Research (3rd ed.). New York: Holt, Rinehart & Winston.

KESSLER, R. C. and GREENBERG, D. F. (1981) Linear Panel Analysis: Models of Quantitative Change. New York: John Wiley.

KIM, K. H. and ROUSH, F. W. (1980) Mathematics for Social Scientists. New York: Elsevier.

KLECKA, W. R. (1980) Discriminant Analysis. Beverly Hills, CA: Sage.

KLEINBAUM, D. G., KUPPER, L. L. and MULLER, K. E. (1988) Applied Regression Analysis and Other Multivariable Methods. Boston: PWS-Kent.

KNOKE, D. and BURKE, P. J. (1989) Log-Linear Models. Beverly Hills, CA: Sage.

KNOKE, D. and HOUT, M. (1976) "Reply to Glenn." American Sociological Review 41: 905-908.

KRAEMER, H.C. and THIEMANN, S. (1987) How Many Subjects? Statistical Power Analysis in Research. Newbury Park, CA: Sage.

LAGRANGE, R. L. and WHITE, H. R. (1985) "Age differences in delinquency: A test of a theory." Criminology 23: 19-45.

LAZARSFELD, P. F. (1955) "The interpretation of statistical relations as a research operation," in P. F. Lazarsfeld and M. Rosenberg (eds.) The Language of Social Research. New York: Free Press.

LEHNEN, R. G. and SKOGAN, W. G. (eds.) (1981) The National Crime Survey: Working Papers. Volume I: Current and Historical Perspectives. Washington, DC: Department of Justice.

LEWIS, O. (1951) Life in a Mexican Village: Tepoztlan Restudied. Urbana: University of Illinois Press.

LIKER, J. K., AUGUSTYNIAK, S. and DUNCAN, G. J. (1985) "Panel data and models of change: A comparison of first difference and conventional two-wave models." Social Science Research 14: 80-101.

LINDEMAN, R. H., MERENDA, P. F. and GOLD, R. Z. (1980) Introduction to Bivariate and Multivariate Analysis. Glenview, IL: Scott, Foresman.

LLOYD, L., ARMOUR, P. K. and SMITH, R. J. (1987) "Suicide in Texas: A cohort analysis of trends in suicide rates, 1945-1980." Suicide and Life-Threatening Behavior 17: 205-217.

MAHAJAN, V. and PETERSON, R. A. (1985) Models for Innovation Diffusion. Beverly Hills, CA: Sage.

MARKUS, G. B. (1979) Analyzing Panel Data. Beverly Hills, CA: Sage.

MARTIN, E. (1983) "Surveys as social indicators: Problems in monitoring trends," in P. H. Rossi, J. D. Wright, and A. B. Anderson (eds.) Handbook of Survey Research. Orlando, FL: Academic Press.

MASON, K. O., MASON, W. M., WINSBOROUGH, H. H. and POOLE, W. K. (1973) "Some methodological issues in cohort analysis of archival data." American Sociological Review 38: 242-258.

MASON, W. M., MASON, K. O., and WINSBOROUGH, H. H. (1976) "Reply to Glenn." American Sociological Review 41: 904-905.

MAULDIN, W. P. and BERELSON, B. (1978) "Conditions of fertility decline in developing countries: 1965-1975." Studies in Family Planning 9: 89-145.

McCLEARY, R. and HAY, R. A., Jr. (1980) Applied Time Series Analysis for the Social Sciences. Beverly Hills, CA: Sage.

McCORD, J. (1983) "A longitudinal study of aggression and antisocial behavior." in K. T. Van Dusen and S. A. Mednick (eds.) Prospective Studies of Crime and Delinquency. Boston: Kluwer-Nijhoff.

McKEOWN, T. (1976) The Modern Rise of Population. London: Edward Arnold.

McKEOWN, T. and RECORD, R. (1962) "Reasons for the decline of mortality in England and Wales during the 19th century." Population Studies 16: 94-122.

McNEILL, W. H. (1976) Plagues and Peoples. New York: Anchor/Doubleday.

MEAD, M. (1928) Coming of Age in Western Samoa: A Psychological Study of Primitive Youth for Western Civilization. New York: William Morrow.

MENARD, S. (1983) "Reliability issues in international comparisons of inequality of income." Paper presented at the annual meeting of the Western Social Science Association.

MENARD, S. (1986) "A research note on international comparisons of inequality of income." Social Forces 3: 778-793.

MENARD, S. (1987a) "Short term trends in crime and delinquency: A comparison of UCR, NCS, and self-report data." Justice Quarterly 4: 455-474.

MENARD, S. (1987b) "Fertility, development, and family planning, 1970-1980: An analysis of cases weighted by population." Studies in Comparative International Development 22: 103-127.

MENARD, S. (1990) "Cross-national models of fertility, family planning, and development: Testing for reciprocal effects." Studies in Comparative International Development 25: 60-90.

MENARD, S. and ELLIOTT, D. S. (1990a) "Longitudinal and cross-sectional data collection and analysis in the study of crime and delinquency." Justice Quarterly 7: 11-55.

MENARD, S. and ELLIOTT, D. S. (1990b) "Self-reported offending, maturational reform, and the Easterlin hypothesis.." Journal of Quantitative Criminology 6: 237-267.

MENARD, S., ELLIOTT, D. S. and HUIZINGA, D. (1989) "The dynamics of deviant behavior: A national survey progress report." National Youth Survey Report No. 49. Boulder, CO: Institute of Behavioral Science.

MENARD, S. and HUIZINGA, D. (1989) "Age, period, and cohort size effects on self-reported alcohol, marijuana, and polydrug use: Results from the National Youth Survey." Social Science Research 18: 174-194.

MENSCH, B. S. and KANDEL, D. B. (1988) "Underreporting of substance use in a national longitudinal youth cohort: Individual and interviewer effects." Public Opinion Quarterly 52: 100-124.

MURRAY, G. F. and ERICKSON, P. G. (1987) "Cross-sectional versus longitudinal research: An empirical comparison of projected and subsequent criminality." Social Science Research 16: 107-118.

78

NAGEL, E. (1961) The Structure of Science. New York: Harcourt, Brace, and World.
NAMBOODIRI, K. and SUCHINDRAN, C. M. (1987) Life Table Techniques and Their Applications. Orlando, FL: Academic Press.
NEWCOMB, M. D. and BENTLER, P. M. (1988) Consequences of Adolescent Drug Use: Impact on the Lives of Young Adults. Newbury Park, CA: Sage.
NOTESTEIN, F. W. (1945) "Population: The long view," in T. W. Schultz (ed.) Food for the World. Chicago: University of Chicago Press.
PALMORE, E. (1978) "When can age, period, and cohort be separated?" Social Forces 57: 282-295.
PETERS, H. E. (1988) "Retrospective versus panel data in analyzing lifecycle events." Journal of Human Resources 23: 488-573.
PIAGET, J. (1948) The Moral Judgment of the Child. New York: Free Press.
PIAGET, J. (1951) The Child's Conception of the World. New York: Humanities Press.
PIAGET, J. (1952) The Origins of Intelligence in Children. New York: International University Press.
PLATT, J. R. (1964) "Strong inference." Science 146: 347-353.
PLEWIS, I. (1985) Analyzing Change: Measurement and Explanation Using Longitudinal Data. Chichester, England: Wiley.
POPULATION REFERENCE BUREAU (1989) "Speaking graphically: When did you say you were born, Miss?" Population Today 9:2.
PRESIDENT'S COMMISSION ON LAW ENFORCEMENT AND THE ADMINISTRATION OF JUSTICE (1967) The Challenge of Crime in a Free Society. Washington, DC: Government Printing Office.
REDFIELD, R. (1930) Tepoztlan: A Mexican Village. Chicago: University of Chicago Press.
RICHARDSON, L. F. (1960) Arms and Insecurity. Pittsburgh: Boxwood Press.
ROBEY, B. (1989) "Two hundred years and counting: The 1990 census." Population Bulletin 4(1): 1-43.
RODGERS, W. L. (1982a) "Estimable functions of age, period, and cohort effects." American Sociological Review 47: 774-787.
RODGERS, W. L. (1982b) "Reply to comment by Smith, Mason, and Fienberg." American Sociological Review 47: 793-796.
ROSSI, P. H. and FREEMAN, H. E. (1989) Evaluation: A Systematic Approach (4th ed.). Newbury Park, CA: Sage.
ROSTOW, W. W. (1960) The Stages of Economic Growth: A Non-Communist Manifesto. Cambridge, MA: Cambridge University Press.
RUBIN, Z. and MITCHELL, C. (1978) "Couples research as couples counseling: Some unintended effects of studying close relationships." American Psychologist 31: 17-25.
RYDER, N. B. (1965) "The cohort as a concept in the study of social change." American Sociological Review 30: 843-861.
SAYRS, L. W. (1989) Pooled Time Series Analysis. Newbury Park, CA: Sage.
SCHMIDT, P. and WITTE, A. D. (1988) Predicting Recidivism Using Survival Models. New York: Springer-Verlag.
SCHOENBERG, R. (1977) "Dynamic models and cross-sectional data: The consequences of dynamic misspecification." Social Science Research 6: 133-144.
SCHWEINHART, L. J. and WEIKART, D. P. (1980) Young Children Grow Up: The Effects of the Perry Preschool Program on Youths Through Age 15. Ypsilanti, MI: High/Scope Educational Research Foundation.

SHELDON, E. B. and MOORE, W. E. (1968) Indicators of Social Change: Concepts and Measurements. New York: Russell Sage.

SHRYOCK, H. S., SIEGEL, J. and Associates (1976) The Methods and Materials of Demography. Condensed edition by E. G. Stockwell. New York: Academic Press.

SIEGEL, S. (1956) Nonparametric Statistics for the Behavioral Sciences. New York: McGraw-Hill.

SIMON, H. J. (1954) "Spurious correlation: A causal interpretation." Journal of the American Statistical Association 49: 467-479.

SIMS, C. A. (1972) "Money, income, and causality." American Economic Review 62: 540-552.

SKOGAN, W. G. (1976) "The victims of crime: Some national survey findings," in A. L. Guenther (ed.) Criminal Behavior and Social Systems (2nd ed.). Chicago: Rand McNally.

SMITH, H. L., MASON, W. M. and FIENBERG, S. E. (1982) "More chimeras of the age-period cohort accounting framework: Comment on Rodgers." American Sociological Review 47: 787-793.

SORENSON, A. M., BROWNFIELD, D. and CARLSON, V. (1989) "Adult reports of juvenile delinquency: A research note on the reliability of a retrospective design." Sociological Spectrum 9: 227-237.

TAEUBER, C. (ed.) (1981) "America enters the eighties: Some social indicators." The Annals of the American Academy of Political and Social Science 453: 1-253.

THOMLINSON, R. (1976) Population Dynamics: Causes and Consequences of World Population Change (2nd ed.). New York: Random House.

THOMPSON, W. S. (1929) "Population." American Journal of Sociology 34: 959-975.

THOMSEN, D. E. (1987) "In the beginning was quantum mechanics: Cosmologists take a chance on a quantum universe." Science News 131: 346-347.

TOLNAY, S. E. and CHRISTENSON, R. L. (1984) "The effects of social setting and family planning programs on recent fertility declines in developing countries: A reassessment." Sociology and Social Research 69: 72-89.

TSUI, A. O. and BOGUE, D. J. (1978) "Declining world fertility: Trends, causes, implications." Population Bulletin 33 (4): 2-55.

U.S. DEPARTMENT OF JUSTICE (1988) "Criminal victimization 1987." Bureau of Justice Statistics Bulletin. Washington, DC: Bureau of Justice Statistics.

U.S. DEPARTMENT OF JUSTICE (1989) "Households touched by crime, 1988." Bureau of Justice Statistics Bulletin. Washington, DC: Bureau of Justice Statistics.

VAN DE GEER, J. P. (1971) Introduction to Multivariate Analysis for the Social Sciences. San Francisco: W. H. Freeman.

VAN DE WALLE, E. and KNODEL, J. (1980) "Europe's fertility transition: New evidence and lessons for today's developing world." Population Bulletin 34(6): 2-40.

VIGDERHOUS, G. (1977) "Forecasting sociological phenomena: Application of Box-Jenkins methodology to suicide rates," in K. F. Schuessler (ed.) Sociological Methodology 1978. San Francisco: Jossey-Bass.

WALL, W. D. and WILLIAMS, H. L. (1970) Longitudinal Studies and the Social Sciences. London: Heinemann.

WEI, W. W. S. (1990) Time Series Analysis: Univariate and Multivariate Methods. Redwood City, CA: Addison-Wesley.

WEIKART, D. P., BOND, J. T. and McNEIL, J. T. (1978) The Ypsilanti Perry Preschool Project: Preschool Years and Longitudinal Results Through Fourth Grade. Ypsilanti, MI: High/Scope Educational Research Foundation.

WEIS, J. G. (1986) "Issues in the measurement of criminal careers," in A. Blumstein, J. Cohen, J. A. Roth, and C. A. Visher (eds.) Criminal Careers and "Career Criminals," Volume II. Washington, DC: National Academy Press.

WETZEL, R. D., REICH, T., MURPHY, G. E., PROVINCE, M. and MILLER, J. P. (1987) "The changing relationship between age and suicide rates: Cohort effect, period effect, or both?" Psychiatric Developments 3: 174-218.

WILDT, A. R. and AHTOLA, O. T. (1978) Analysis of Covariance. Beverly Hills, CA: Sage.

WILLIAMS, J. and GOLD, M. (1972) "From delinquent behavior to official delinquency." Social Problems 20: 209-229.

WILLIAMSON, J. B., KARP, D. A., DALPHIN, J. R. and GRAY, P. S. (1982) The Research Craft: An Introduction to Social Research Methods. Boston: Little, Brown.

WOFFORD, S. (1989) "A preliminary analysis of the relationship between employment and delinquency/crime for adolescents and young adults." National Youth Survey Report No. 50. Boulder, CO: Institute of Behavioral Science.

WRIGHT, R. E. (1989) "The Easterlin hypothesis and European fertility rates." Population and Development Review 15: 107-122.

WRIGHT, R. E. and MAXIM, P. S. (1987) "Canadian fertility trends: A further test of the Easterlin hypothesis." Canadian Review of Sociology and Anthropology 24: 339-357.

YAMAGUCHI, K. and KANDEL, D. B. (1984a) "Patterns of drug use from adolescence to young adulthood II: Sequences of progression." American Journal of Public Health 74: 668-672.

YAMAGUCHI, K. and KANDEL, D. B. (1984b) "Patterns of drug use from adolescence to young adulthood III: Predictors of progression." American Journal of Public Health 74: 673-681.

ZAZZO, R. (1967) "Diversite, realite, et mirages de la methode longitudinale: Rapport introducif au symposium des etudes longitudinales." Enfance, Volume 2. Cited in Wall and Williams (1970).

ZELLER, R. A. and CARMINES, E. G. (1980) Measurement in the Social Sciences: The Link Between Theory and Data. Cambridge, England: Cambridge University Press.

ABOUT THE AUTHOR

SCOTT MENARD is a Research Associate in the Institute of Behavioral Science at the University of Colorado, Boulder. He received his Ph.D. from the University of Colorado in 1981. His publications include *Perspectives on Population* (with Elizabeth W. Moen), *Multiple Problem Youth* (with Delbert S. Elliott and David Huizinga), and papers on demography, crime, delinquency, and criminal justice. His present research interests include the analysis of short-term trends in illegal behavior, temporal order analysis, and the analysis of age, period, and cohort effects.